The Mystery of Jesus

THE MEDITATIONS OF ARCHBISHOP MARCEL LEFEBVRE

ANGELUS PRESS
2918 Tracy Avenue, Kansas City, Missouri 64109

This work is a translation by Miss Anne Stinnett of the Angelus Press staff of *Le Mystère de Notre Seigneur Jésus Christ*, published by Clovis Publishers in 1995. It was serialized in *The Angelus* from May 1996 to January 1999.

ANGELUS PRESS
2918 TRACY AVENUE
KANSAS CITY, MISSOURI 64109
PHONE (816) 753-3150
FAX (816) 753-3557
ORDER LINE 1-800-966-7337

ISBN 1-892331-02-0

FIRST PRINTING—May 2000

Printed in the United States of America

Library of Congress Cataloging-in-Publication Data

Lefebvre, Marcel 1905-
[Mystère de notre Seigneur Jésus Christ. English]
The mystery of Our Lord Jesus Christ / Marcel Lefebvre
p. cm.
Includes bibliographical references.
ISBN 0-892331-02-0 (pbk.)
1. Jesus Christ–Person and offices. I. Title
BT202 .L4312 2000
232–dc21

00–029324

Contents

Notice to the Reader

These pages substantially transcribe the series of spiritual conferences that Archbishop Lefebvre gave to the seminarians of the St. Pius X Seminary at Écône, Switzerland, from November 28, 1977 to March 29, 1979. The Archbishop himself entitled them, "The Mystery of Our Lord Jesus Christ." This series of conferences followed some preparatory conferences with the theme of the call to holiness and the dispositions necessary to advance in the spiritual life.

One can easily understand that the series of conferences on the mystery of Christ was very often interrupted by the frequent trips of the Archbishop, as well as by other conferences given on current events and other themes. This explains the numerous repetitions by which the prelate resumed the thread of his long exposition. These recapitulations are, however, neither unhelpful nor unpleasant to read; they always bring a new approach to the mystery, in the same way that looking at the different facets of a diamond allows the beholder to admire its sparkling beauty without ever exhausting it. This manner of exposition by repetitions and advances corresponds, moreover, to the contemplative spirit that was Archbishop Lefebvre's.

St. Thomas held from St. Denis the distinction of three movements in the act of contemplation: circular, oblique, and straight. The latter, like the flight of the lark rising and descending above its nest, is the manner of the mind that rises from sensible things to spiritual things and vice versa in order to illustrate divine things with the help of terrestrial things. The oblique motion is that of the mind that uses divine illumination to reason on the truths of faith, proceeding from principles to theological conclusions and inversely, like the dove that flies from one branch of a tree to that of another, lower or higher. Finally, there is the circular motion, uniform around a center, when the soul takes in with one glance several aspects of a divine truth, and, as a circular movement without beginning and without end, circumscribes the mystery, like the eagle soaring in the heights describes a large circle keeping a panoramic sight of the whole without taking its eye off the center.[1]

It is undoubtedly this circular movement of contemplation that allowed Archbishop Lefebvre to successively contemplate all the aspects of the mystery of the Incarnate Word like an eagle contemplating in detail and in general the entire region over which it flies....Archbishop Lefebvre sees in a remarkable manner the implication of the divine processions in the divine missions, as well as the interconnection of the mystery of the Holy Trinity and that of the Incarnation, a connection that he resumes by these words which his listeners heard so often from his mouth that they remain engraved in their memories: "We have no other God than our Lord Jesus Christ!"

If the flight patterns of the lark and the dove are like the proceedings of the theologian, that of the eagle belongs to the contemplative, and the first two are ordered to the latter, as teaches Fr. Garrigou-Lagrange following St. Thomas,[2] saying "theology is a science subordinate to the science of God and the blessed." This implies that the best theologian will also be a contemplative. Without neglecting theological reasoning, Archbishop Lefebvre often prefers to it the short cut revealed by the contemplative's in-

---

1 *Cf.* St. Thomas Aquinas, *Summa Theologica*, II-II, Q. 180, A. 6.
2 *Op. cit.*, I, Q. 1, A. 2.

tuition, or the admiring gaze, or, finally, the simple silence of one who can find no words to express what he sees. Standing before the Holy of holies, he can only fall silent and tell us, "It is a mystery," "there is the mystery." Our minds, inclined to ratiocinate, might feel some dissatisfaction, but the opposite is true: what a purification!

Archbishop Lefebvre's exposition is not meant to be a complete treatise of Christology; certain aspects of the mystery have not been developed, such as, for example, the plenitude of grace in Christ, or the consequences of the capital grace of Jesus Christ for the Mystical Body, or even the priesthood of Christ. These aspects are never entirely absent, but they are continually assimilated to the central truth of the hypostatic union, to the dogma of the divinity of Christ which constitutes the essence of the subject. The great merit of these conferences, in fact, is that they focus on several great principles which the speaker delights in repeating—to the point of satiety, one might say—like the apostle St. John who would repeat incessantly to the disciples the precept of fraternal charity, "because it is the precept of the Lord, and if one keeps it, it is enough." Is it not, after all, the touchstone of the great masters to know how to recapitulate everything in a few principles, the simplest, the most luminous, and the highest?

Like St. Paul and St. Pius X, Archbishop Lefebvre loves to "re-establish all things in Christ" (Eph. 1:10), and, more particularly, to bring back everything to this capital truth, the divinity of our Lord Jesus Christ. This truth, which supposes the mystery of the Blessed Trinity with the processions and missions of the divine Persons, is never separated from its concrete implications. On the contrary, man of action that he was as well as contemplative, Archbishop Lefebvre emphasizes the practical consequences of the divinity of Jesus Christ: His universal royalty, His social reign, fought against by the liberals. As a missionary full of faith, he sees in the person of the Man-God the unique Savior, the founder of the one true religion, the head of His unique mystical body which is the Catholic Church, the captain of the unique ark "outside of which it is impossible to be saved."[3] He sees in the divinity of our Lord Jesus Christ the annihilation of ecumenism and of religious liberty, against which he does not let pass any opportunity of inveighing.

A pastor of souls, Archbishop Lefebvre does not fail to investigate the spiritual avenues of the dogma. The contemplation of the soul of Jesus Christ is the best means of sanctification, since His soul is, by His virtues, the model of our spiritual life, and by His plenitude of grace the cause of our salvation. He shows in the Man-God, not the singular being who constitutes the exception, but the normal man, the perfect man, on the model of whom we have been created and recreated in justice. The simple fact that we have the same sanctifying grace that our Lord Jesus Christ has (even if it is not in plenitude, of course) should throw us into admiration, not of man—some abstract and transcendental man[4]—but of the new man, "who according to God is created in justice and holiness of truth" (Eph. 4:24), on the model of Christ. If the mystery of the Incarnation is ordered to the Redemption of the human race, as Archbishop Lefebvre holds following St. Thomas, that does not mean that He is subordinated to the good of man, for, ultimately, it is ordered to the manifestation of the total

---

3 *Cf.* Pius XII, encyclical letter *Humani Generis, etc.*

4 Such is man according to the "new theology," the theology of de Lubac, Rahner, and John Paul II, the man to which would be ordered the mystery of the Incarnate Word, in order to manifest the dignity of the human person!

Christ, to the glorification of the Man-God in the members of His mystical body, as St. Paul teaches. "All things were created by Him and for Him," he says of our Lord (Col. 1:16). He is "Alpha and Omega, the beginning and the end" of everything, in His very mystery of Man-God (Apoc. 1:8). Far from being anthropocentric, like the false spirituality of the modernists, our spirituality is Christocentric, entirely centered on the adorable Person of our Lord Jesus Christ.

In preparing the transcription for publication, we have had to alter the text slightly, which, without harming the spoken style of the lecturer, aims at observing as closely as possible the exactness of diction required for a written text, but which is less necessary when the varying intonations of the voice give to spoken expressions their appropriate significance. Likewise, we have tried to order the ideas which the orator, under the influence of inspiration, has not always been able to clearly delineate. Sometimes we have completed the abundant citations that Archbishop Lefebvre makes of the authors whom he appreciated, like Abbot Marmion or Fr. Bonsirven, *etc.* So doing, we believe that we have betrayed neither the thought nor the expression of the Archbishop, persuaded as we are that he himself would have carefully reviewed the written text of his conferences, if he had been able to, for their publication. Thus we have divided the exposition into short chapters which did not equal in length the time of each conference, but which follow their exact order. Finally, we have provided abundant footnotes, most drawn from approved authors, often St. Thomas Aquinas and St. Augustine, in order to illustrate as well as possible Archbishop Lefebvre's ideas and to show their deep roots in the Church's tradition.

A word needs to be said about the sources from which the lecturer drew. Besides St. Thomas Aquinas, his preferred master, he drew inspiration from Fr. Joseph Bonsirven, S.J., in his work *Les enseignements de Jesus Christ* [*The Teachings of Jesus Christ*];[5] but this takes nothing away from the essential part of these conferences which is owed to the reflection, the personal research, the original construction, the constant reference to holy Scripture, and finally, as we have said, to an incessant contemplation of the mystery of our Lord Jesus Christ.

There is another source, more distant and more diffuse but nonetheless present and important in these conferences. One could even say that they had their origin in the reading, certainly attentive and fruitful, which the then seminarian, abbé Marcel Lefebvre, made of it in the seminary. It concerns a work which he no longer had at hand when he was preparing these conferences at Écône: a little book in two volumes of 215 and 179 pages, entitled *La psychologie du Christ*, by the Canon Jean Arthur Chollet, Doctor in Theology, and Professor at the School of Theology of Lille, published by Letheilleux in 1903.

It was only a year before the Archbishop's death that a correspondent, Mr. Paul del Perrugia, wrote to him suggesting that he reprint the work, of which he possessed a copy. Here is what Archbishop Lefebvre wrote him:

> Écône, March 13, 1990
>
> Dear Sir,
>
> Providence is good to encourage you to write me about the treasure which is the book of Msgr. Chollet on *The Psychology of Christ*.
>
> Having much appreciated it while I was a seminarian at

5 Collection *Verbum salutis*, Beauchesne, Paris, 1946.

> Rome between 1923-1930, I have often looked for it in libraries. It is simply not to be found.
>
> That is to let you know how much your letter cheered me and awakened a hope that it might be possible to reprint it...
>
> I knew Mgr. Chollet, a great mind in the service of the Catholic faith, without compromise.
>
> Thank you cordially for your communication, ...

The spiritual affinity existing between the seminarian and the theology professor of Lille found its completion a few years later, when Mgr. Chollet, who had become Bishop of Verdun and then Archbishop of Cambrai, consecrated Mgr. Quillet, who consecrated Mgr. Lecomte, who consecrated Mgr. Liénart, from whom Msgr. Lefebvre would receive in turn the fullness of the priesthood, becoming thus the great-great-grandson of Mgr. Chollet in the episcopacy.

We ask of God for the readers of this work many graces and spiritual joys, for if St. Paul himself asked the Lord for the graces necessary to allow him to expose the mystery of our Lord Jesus Christ "in whom are hid all the treasures of wisdom and knowledge" (Eph. 2:3), then how much more have we need of abundant graces to be able to receive this teaching and penetrate, in our turn, "the unsearchable riches of Christ" (Eph. 3:8).

+Bernard Tissier de Mallerais
Menzingen, 22 February 1995
Feast of the Chair of St. Peter

AUTHOR'S INTRODUCTION

According to the means that the good God grants me, I would like to try to present to your understanding the mystery of our Lord Jesus Christ. It is always our Lord who is the center and heart of our life, and Who will be so eternally. For it is by Him and in Him that we are able to live by grace, live in charity, and prepare our eternity. There is no other way.

When we poor sinners weigh what we are, always tempted by our weaknesses and by the wounds of original sin to favor rather the disorder within, we need to find not only a model, but also the One who is the cause of the order to be re-established. Our Lord is not only our model, He is also the cause of our resurrection, the cause of our sanctification; it is in Him that we truly find all that we need for our sanctification.

The Catholic Church presents us this perfect man in our Lord Jesus Christ. The more we contemplate Him, the more we frequent Him by all the means placed at our disposition by our Lord Himself: holy Church, the holy sacrifice of the Mass, and especially the Holy Eucharist, the more we should be able to penetrate the mystery that is our Lord Jesus Christ. Indeed, here is after all a great mystery! St. Paul repeats this constantly. It is what he teaches in a special manner to all those to whom he is sent.

> With this in mind, I fall on my knees; I, Paul, of whom Jesus Christ has made a prisoner for the love of you Gentiles. You will have been told how God planned to give me a special grace for preaching to you; how a revelation taught me the secret I have been setting out briefly here; briefly, yet so as to let you see how well I have mastered this secret of Christ's. It was never made known to any human being in past ages, as it has now been revealed by the Spirit to his holy apostles and

> prophets, and it is this: that through the gospel preaching the Gentiles are to win the same inheritance, to be made part of the same body, to share the same divine promise, in Christ Jesus. With what grace God gives me (and he gives it in all the effectiveness of his power), I am a minister of that gospel; on me, least as I am of all the saints, he has bestowed this privilege, of making known to the Gentiles the unfathomable riches of Christ, of publishing to the world the plan of this mystery, kept hidden from the beginning of time in the all-creating mind of God. The principalities and powers of heaven are to see, now, made manifest in the Church, the subtlety of God's wisdom; such is his eternal purpose, centered in Christ Jesus our Lord (Eph. 3:1-11).

This is truly St. Paul's great pre-occupation: to make known to the Gentiles the great mystery of Christ. For it is true as we profess in our Faith, that our Lord Jesus Christ is the Man-God, yet in the mystery of this union of God with human nature, it is obvious that we have much to meditate on. For this man who walked Palestine and lived at Nazareth for thirty years was God. A very extraordinary thing. How can God be in a human body, in a simple limited human soul?! Is it obvious that God can do without a human person and of Himself directly assume a soul and a body? It is clearly a mystery, because we cannot completely succeed in understanding this absolutely stupefying reality, the Incarnation of God. And nonetheless it is in this mystery that our salvation lies. It is in this mystery that the reason for the existence of creation lies.

CHAPTER1

SON OF GOD

Let me try, as far as it is possible, to speak of the mystery of our Lord Jesus Christ.

If St. Paul himself says that he prays God to inspire him with fitting words to speak of the mystery, then it is clear that we are touching upon a subject that is truly mysterious and yet so real, so important, that ultimately, it is the heart of our life, the object of our meditations, the source of our sanctification. By the Faith, we believe and confess that He is God and Man. Nevertheless, it is still good to reread the Scriptures that treat this question so that our minds can be impressed by this truth.

First of all, it is our Lord Jesus Christ Himself who affirmed it. Though it is true that our Lord did not reveal immediately that He was the Son of God, it is not correct to say, as the modernists do, that He was unaware He was the true Son of God consubstantial with the Father and the Holy Ghost, but that by a sort of new awareness of Himself simply knew of His special quality of son of God, and this only at the end of His public life. Obviously, all of this is completely false.[6] At the end of His life our Lord proclaimed his divinity before Caiphas:

---

6 As early as the fifth century, this same heresy into which the modernists now fall was denounced by St. Fulgentius (468-533). He wrote: "It is quite impossible and totally foreign to the Catholic faith to say that the soul of Christ was not fully conscious of His divinity, with which we believe that it made but one Person" (Letter 12, ch. 3, no. 26). "But whereas the divinity knew itself as such because it was naturally such, the soul knew the divinity without itself being divine...." (Letter 4, ch. 3, no. 31).

> The chief priests and elders and all the council tried to find false testimony against Jesus, such as would compass his death. But they could find none, although many came forward falsely accusing him; until at last two false accusers came forward who declared, This man said, I have power to destroy the temple of God and raise it again in three days. Then the high priest stood up, and asked him, Hast thou no answer to make to the accusations these men bring against thee?...Jesus was silent; and the high priest said to him openly, I adjure thee by the living God to tell us whether thou art the Christ, the Son of God? Jesus answered: Thy own lips have said it. And moreover I tell you this; you will see the Son of Man again, when he is seated at the right hand of power, and comes on the clouds of heaven....And they answered: The penalty is death (Mt. 26:61,62,64,66).

So it is clear: When our Lord publicly proclaimed His divinity, the high priest judged it blasphemy, that this man made Himself God, and so deserved death. This text is a solemn affirmation by our Lord that He is truly the Son of God, and that one day He will be seen coming on the clouds of heaven. There is another significant passage, the episode of the Transfiguration.

> Six days afterwards Jesus took Peter and James and his brother John with him, and led them up to a high mountain where they were alone. And he was transfigured in their presence...(Mt. 17).

We should think and believe the Transfiguration should have been our Lord's normal state. What was abnormal, was that He was not habitually transfigured, since He possessed the beatific vision. From the instant of His birth–rather, the moment His soul was created–it enjoyed the beatific vision. Thus the effects of the beatific vision should have been felt by His body, as for the elect, whose bodies will be transfigured and will have all the properties of resurrected bodies, luminous and shining like the sun. This will be an effect of the beatific vision, of the glory of God in souls. Our Lord should normally have had such a body. But He wanted to live like other men, and it was by a miracle that He did not habitually have a transfigured body.

> And he was transfigured in their presence, his face shining like the sun, and his garments becoming white as snow; and all at once they had sight of Moses and Elias conversing with him. Then Peter said aloud to Jesus, Lord, it is well that we should be here; if it pleases thee, let us make three booths in this place, one for thee, one for Moses and one for Elias. Even before he had finished speaking, a shining cloud overshadowed them. And now, there was a voice which said to them out of the cloud, This is my beloved son, in whom I am well pleased; to him, then, listen. The disciples, when they heard it, fell on their faces, overcome with fear; but Jesus came near and roused them with his touch; Arise, he said, do not be afraid. And they lifted up their eyes, and saw no man there but Jesus only.
>
> And as they were coming down from the mountain, Jesus warned them, do not tell anybody of what you have seen, until the Son of Man has risen from the dead (Mt. 17:1-9).

Here again is a proof of the divinity of our Lord. It is God Himself who affirms it: our Lord is His Son "in whom I am well pleased." But before that, there is another event in the public life of our Lord:

> So he reached the other shore, in the country of the Gerasenes; and here he was met by two possessed creatures who came out of the rock tombs, so exceedingly fierce that none could pass along that road. And at once they cried aloud, Why dost thou meddle with us, Jesus, Son of God (Mt. 8:28ff)?

The devils themselves confess the divinity of our Lord Jesus Christ. They express their fear: "Have you come here to torment us before the appointed time?" They pray to Jesus: "If you chase us hence, send us into the herd of swine."

Jesus grants their prayer. Does this testimony of the devils mean that they believe in His divinity? St. Thomas Aquinas (*Summa Theologica* III, Q.44, A.1) answers:

> Christ made Himself known to the devils, not by His eter-

> nal life, but rather by certain temporal effects of His power. At first, seeing Christ hungry after His fast, they concluded that He was not the Son of God. But then at the spectacle of His miracles they came by conjecture to believe, but not with certitude, that He was the Son of God. If in the end the devil incited the Jews to crucify Christ, it was not because he did not recognize His divinity, but because he did not foresee that by His death Christ would definitively vanquish him.

So much for the testimony of the devils. One could, of course, multiply the examples drawn from Scripture. In general, the Gospels constitute the greatest proof of the divinity of our Lord Jesus Christ, as well as His humanity.

CHAPTER 2

THE WORD MADE FLESH

It is St. John who, in his Gospel, gives even more emphasis than the other Evangelists to the divinity of our Lord, which he affirms. It is enough to reread the first chapter of the Gospel according to St. John. We can never read it too often; it is one of the most beautiful pages of the Gospel, deep and consoling.

It used to be that the priest or bishop recited this gospel while returning to the sacristy after Mass. It was his way of making his thanksgiving. Later, the Church required the priest to recite this prayer at the altar before the faithful:

> In the beginning was the Word: and the Word was with God: and the Word was God. The same was in the beginning with God. All things were made by him: and without him was made nothing that was made. In him was life: and the life was the light of men. And the light shineth in darkness: and the darkness did not comprehend it.

In this way St. John presents to us God's eternity, creation, and also sin:

> There was a man sent from God, whose name was John. This man came for a witness, to give testimony of the light, that all men might believe through him. He was not the light, but was to give testimony of the light. That was the true light, which enlighteneth every man that cometh into this world. He was in the world: and the world was made by him: and the world knew him not. He came unto his own: and his own received him not.

This is a general statement, obviously; later on St. John makes the distinction between these and "those who received him." But let us always keep in mind this affirmation: *Omnia per ipsum facta sunt*, which is included in the *Creed*. We must never forget nor dissociate this omnipotence from our Lord, Creator.

Our Lord is God, and there is but one God; there are not three Gods, there is only one. Consequently, God the Father, God the Son, and God the Holy Ghost created the world. The Word created the world: "All things were made by him," hence by our Lord. For there are not two persons in our Lord, but one, and this person is the person of the Word of God, the person of God the Son.

This thought should be ever-present in our minds:

> But as many as received him, he gave them power to be made the sons of God, to them that believe in his name. Who are born, not of blood, nor of the will of the flesh, nor of the will of man, but of God. And the Word was made flesh and dwelt among us...

St. John is surely alluding to the Transfiguration when he writes:

> And we saw his glory, the glory as it were of the only begotten of the Father, full of grace and truth.

Then he recounts the witness of St. John the Baptist who cries out:

> This was he of whom I spoke: He that shall come after me is preferred before me: because he was before me.

These words of the Baptist constitute another affirmation of the divinity of our Lord Jesus Christ. Our Lord, he says, "was before me." He was before him, because it was our Lord who had created him:

> And of his fullness we all have received: and grace for grace.

There is no grace, then, that comes to us outside of our Lord Jesus Christ.

All these words are of prime importance because they establish the basis of our faith, the principles of our action in our daily life. All the errors which are spread around nowadays, and which make believe that there is another way of salvation other than our Lord Jesus Christ and outside the Catholic religion go expressly against these affirmations of the Gospel, and are explicitly against our Lord Jesus Christ.

Documents coming from the Dutch Bishops' Conference speak of ways of salvation in the non-Christian religions. Absurd. There are no means of salvation outside the Catholic religion founded by our Lord Jesus Christ. Outside the Church there is no salvation. It is a dogma of our faith. Why? Because supernatural grace comes only from the Church. Even those graces which might attain adherents of other religions would come from our Lord Jesus Christ, and consequently from His Church, thanks to the prayer of the Church, the mystical spouse of our Lord who is united to Him and cannot be separated from Him. It is by the intermediary of the Catholic Church that graces are distributed to those who would receive them outside of it.

Undoubtedly, there are souls that are saved and which are not part of the visible structure of the Church, but which belong invisibly to the Church, the mystical body of Christ. The popes have affirmed this. However, undoubtedly this does not occur frequently. The Church must be missionary in order to bring its graces to those who have not received them. If everyone received grace outside the Church, and even if that were by the mediation of the Church, we would not need to be missionaries. It is impossible to be saved by the practice of false religions or by beliefs that are contrary to Church doctrine. It is impossible to be saved by error, by taking a direction opposed to the Holy Ghost, to the Wisdom of God and to the way by which God chose to save us, which is essentially His Incarnation:

> Grace and truth came by Jesus Christ. No man hath seen God at any time: the only begotten Son who is in the bosom of the Father, he hath declared him (Jn. 1:17-18).

The mystery of the God-Man is great, clearly; but it is absolutely necessary to meditate on it, and to know the reality, the truth, because this is our faith, our whole life and the life of the world.

Nothing is done in the world that does not relate to our Lord; it is either for Him or against Him, with Him or without Him. Our Lord is the key to the solution of all the problems. There are none here below that are indifferent to our Lord. Men try in vain to work without reference to our Lord, but it is impossible because our Lord is everywhere.[7] He is in everything because He created everything; therefore everything is in His hands. Everything belongs to Him, nothing is outside of Him. Men seek to evade Him, but they cannot because everything is His.

To try to construct human history outside of our Lord Jesus Christ is an absurdity. Our Lord is the center of history. Everything was made by Him and for Him[8] and the only happiness of men and mankind is to be united to our Lord, to live for God by Jesus Christ, because He is God. He has given us the means; this is why He came. St. John says as much in his first epistle, which is also very beautiful:

> That which was from the beginning, which we have heard, which we have seen with our eyes, which we have looked upon and our hands have handled, of the word of life (I Jn. 1:1).

St. John cannot distract his mind from the moments when he touched our Lord, when he rested his head upon His breast during the Last Supper. The scene is anchored in his mind and he will never forget these instants; he lived

---

7 By His divine nature.

8 *Cf.* Col. 1:16.

to the end of his days in thinking of the extraordinary happiness he had known in touching the Word of God:

> For the life was manifested: and we have seen and do bear witness and declare unto you the life eternal, which was with the Father and hath appeared to us.

How magnificent; in a few words St. John places us before the reality:

> The life eternal which I have seen and touched I communicate to you. That which we have seen and have heard, we declare unto you: that you also may have fellowship with us and our fellowship may be with the Father and with his Son Jesus Christ. And these things we write to you, that you may rejoice and your joy may be full.

Undoubtedly, it was only little by little that the Apostles came to recognize the divinity of our Lord. Even at the Ascension, they were still asking when His temporal reign would begin. What notion did they have of this Person who was before them? In fact, they did not fully understand the mystery of our Lord until after Pentecost, after the pouring forth of the Holy Ghost upon them. They drew from it the consequences which appear in their writings. This is what is admirable. Then one understands what St. John wrote in his first epistle:

> I have not written to you as to them that know not the truth, but as to them that know it: and that no lie is of the truth. Who is a liar, but he who denieth that Jesus is the Christ? This is Antichrist, who denieth the Father and the Son. Whosoever denieth the Son, the same hath not the Father. He that confesseth the Son hath the Father also. As for you, let that which you have heard from the beginning abide in you. If that abide in you, which you have heard from the beginning, you also shall abide in the Son and in the Father. And this is the promise which he hath promised us, life everlasting.
> (I Jn. 2:21-25).

He adds and repeats further on:

> By this is the spirit of God known. Every spirit which confesseth that Jesus Christ is come in the flesh is of God. And

every spirit that dissolveth Jesus is not of God. And this is Antichrist, of whom you have heard that he cometh: and he is now already in the world. (I Jn. 4:2-3).

The affirmations of the Apostles and the Evangelists are quite precise: Those who affirm the divinity of our Lord Jesus Christ are of God. Those who deny it are not. The consequences are enormous. Think of the multitudes of people, of all humanity which lives today as the men who lived before. It is in relation to our Lord Jesus Christ and His divinity that the fate of all these men is decided, and so their eternity.

CHAPTER 3

A DIVINE PERSON

St. Paul is the one who has most clearly expressed the grandeur of our Lord Jesus Christ, His power and divinity, especially in the first chapters of the epistles to the Hebrews and to the Colossians. These merit to be reread often.

> In old days, God spoke to our fathers in many ways and by many means, through the prophets; now at last in these times he has spoken to us, with a Son to speak for him; a Son, whom he has appointed to inherit all things, just as it was through him that he created this world of time; a Son, who is the radiance of his Father's splendor, and the full expression of his being; all creation depends, for its support, on his enabling word. Now, making atonement for our sins, he has taken his place on high, at the right hand of God's majesty, superior to the angels in that measure in which the name he has inherited is more excellent than theirs. (Heb. 1:1-4).

The Person in question is indeed the Son, He who atoned for our sins, thus our Lord Jesus Christ and not the Word only. One cannot make a distinction between our Lord Jesus Christ and the Word. Jesus Christ is the Word of God; there is no other person in Him. Undoubtedly, this is difficult to understand. But herein lies, precisely, the mystery of our Lord Jesus Christ, the fact that this very Person, the Person of this man who lived in Palestine, should be the Word of God by whom all things were made. It is this same divine Person who assumes a human nature, with a soul which thinks, reflects, and wills in a human way, for our Lord was a perfect man. He had, then, His human soul. His human thoughts were attributed to

God because there is no other subject of attribution in our Lord than the Word of God, that is, than God.

All the acts accomplished by our Lord, whatever they were, were divine acts because attributable to the Person; He really possessed all the faculties a man has and a body and all his human gifts. St. Paul enlightens us:

> Did God ever say to one of the angels, Thou art my Son, I have begotten thee this day (Ps. 2:7)? And again, He shall find in me a Father and I in him a Son (II Sam. 7:14)? Why, when the time comes for bringing his first-born into the world anew, then, he says, Let all the angels of God worship before him (Ps. 96:7).

What does he say of the angels?

> He will have his angels be like the winds, the servants that wait on him like a flame of fire (Ps. 103:4). And what of the Son? Thy throne, O God, stands firm for ever and ever; the scepter of thy kingship is a rod that rules true. Thou has been a friend to right, an enemy to wrong; and God, thy own God, has given thee an unction to bring thee pride, as none else of thy fellows (Ps. 44:7-8). And elsewhere: Lord, thou has laid the foundations of the earth at its beginning, and the heavens are the work of thy hands. They will perish, but thou wilt remain; they will all be like a cloak that grows threadbare, and thou wilt lay them aside, like a garment, and exchange them for new; but thou art he who never changes, thy years will not come to an end (Ps.101:26-28). Did he ever say to one of the angels, sit on my right hand, while I make thy enemies a foot-stool under thy feet (Ps. 109:1)? What are they, all of them, but spirits apt for service, whom he sends out when the destined heirs of eternal salvation have need of them. (Heb. 1:5-14).

St. Paul clearly insists on the divinity of our Lord Jesus Christ, on His perfection, which is infinitely greater than that of the angels, who are clearly only creatures. With our poor human imagination, it seems difficult to realize that the one to whom the apostles spoke, whom the Blessed Virgin carried in her womb and in her arms, that this Child Jesus is He by whom all things were made.

Placed before the image of the Infant Jesus in the crib, some might be moved to say, "It is not possible, He could not possibly have created the earth; he was just born." To these St. Paul gives the reply: He was just born, yes, but His Person is a divine Person, and this Person is God, the Word of God. It is truly the Word of God who is there present in the crib, who assumes this body and soul. It is the Word of God, it is this divine Person whom we address. When you speak to someone, you address the person. This Person was the Word of God, by whom all was created. How can anyone then say that this Person who is the Word of God made Man is not Saviour, and Priest and King, the three great attributes that this Person gives to this creature of God by the grace of the hypostatic union?[9]

Has any man then the right to be indifferent to the presence of the Word of God in our midst? It is inconceivable. God has willed to come among us; who then has a right to say, "Just let me live my life: I don't need Jesus Christ to live." It is unthinkable, especially since He came to save us from our sins. Consequently, we are all affected because we are all sinners. He came to die on the cross to redeem us from eternal damnation; can anyone then be disinterested? And how can they dare to compare this Person who is our Lord Jesus Christ to Mohammed or Buddha or Luther?... How can a Catholic who has the Faith utter such words? How can they even speak of "the religions, all the religions, the cults" as if they were equal?

Pope Pius VII manifested his indignation when presented with the Constitution of France in which was affirmed the freedom of all the religions. He reacted against the words "all the religions." By these words they were

---

[9] The union of two natures, divine and human, of Jesus Christ in one unique person, the Person of the divine Word. From the fact that this man Jesus Christ, is God, he is necessarily Savior, Priest, and King.

putting the holy religion of God, of our Lord Jesus Christ, on the same level as the heresies and schisms. He was outraged, and he wrote to the Archbishop of Troyes: "Go and see the king. Tell him that it is inadmissible for a Catholic monarch, for a king who calls himself Catholic, to allow the freedom 'of all the religions,' without distinction." The Pope was indignant. This should be the conviction of every Catholic.

It is not possible to be a Catholic and not feel outrage when they speak of "all the religions," placing thereby our Lord on a par with Buddha and all the rest. They do not believe that our Lord is God. They do not believe that it is the Person of God who is before us. Clearly not. Are there several incarnations of God? In Buddha? In Mohammed? In Luther? No, there is only one, in our Lord Jesus Christ. This fact has enormous consequences, and we should sense this in proportion to our belief in the divinity of our Lord Jesus Christ.

What St. John says on this point is very important, as we have seen. It can be summed up in this way: He who affirms that Jesus Christ is God is of God, and he who denies that our Lord Jesus Christ is God is an antichrist (*cf.* I Jn. 2:22). Antichrist! and, consequently, a devil. St. John, for one, had the Faith, and he knew how to draw the consequences.

It can be wondered today if there are any real Catholics left among those who call themselves Catholic, because everyone finds it natural to speak of freedom of religion and the liberty of worship. Yet that cannot be conceded, because it is contrary to the dignity of our Lord Jesus Christ. They will accuse you of being intolerant. How many Catholics think the same thing, even in our own Catholic families?

If you affirm there is only one true religion, the religion of our Lord Jesus Christ, and all the others come from the devil, that they are of the Antichrist because they deny the divinity of our Lord Jesus Christ, they will accuse you of being intolerant. "So, you want to go back to the Middle Ages," they will sneer. No, we only want to restore what is: our Lord is King. The day when He comes suddenly in majesty upon the clouds of heaven they will say, "Ah, indeed, He is King; we did not believe it was possible."

Yes, our Lord is King, and He will be the only one, there shall be none beside Him. People are not able to convince themselves of it. They are infected by liberalism, by the secularism that affects many. Our Lord Jesus Christ is no longer ascribed his true place.

His reign must be established on the earth as in heaven. It is He himself who said so in the prayer that He taught us, the *Our Father*: *Adveniat regnum tuum, fiat voluntas tua sicut in caelo et in terra.* And this must be the object of our prayers, the intention of our sufferings, and the purpose of our life. We must have no rest until our Lord's reign is established. A Catholic whose heart is not animated by this profound desire is not a Catholic. He is not one of the faithful of our Lord Jesus Christ. It suffices to reread these lines:

> Now at last in these times he has spoken to us, with a Son to speak for him; a Son, whom he has appointed to inherit all things, just as it was through him that he created this world of time (Heb. 1:2).

It is Jesus Christ, God by whom all things were created. The Father, the Son and the Holy Ghost are together the Creator of the world.[10] It is by the Word that the Father created the world in the Holy Ghost.

It is not necessary to have recourse to apologetics or to cite exhaustively all the proofs of the divinity and the humanity of our Lord Jesus Christ. What we need most of all for our spiritual life is to affirm our Faith and not prove it, because it reposes upon the authority of God, on the words of our Lord.

We have perhaps too much of a tendency to rationalize our Faith, to find proofs. Undoubtedly, our Faith is reasonable, and there are valid motives for believing; but we have the Faith, it is by Faith that we believe in God our Lord, and we must affirm this Faith.

---

[10] "*Et in unum Dominum Jesum Christum...per quem omnia facta sunt*—And through Him all things were made" (Nicene Creed).

CHAPTER 4

JESUS CHRIST CONSUBSTANTIAL WITH THE FATHER

After going back over the testimonies of the Scriptures, St. Matthew, St. John and St. Paul, it is also good to read again what the Church, especially from the beginning, wanted to affirm concerning the divinity of our Lord Jesus Christ. This is contained in particular in the three great professions of Faith which are the Apostles' Creed, the Niceen Creed, and the Athanasian Creed. They constitute the fundamental summary of our Faith.

The reading of the first two symbols of the Faith allows us to measure the importance the apostles placed on the mystery of the Incarnation, the mystery of our Lord Jesus Christ, which is truly the principal object of our *Credo.* As Jesus is God, all that is said of God necessarily applies to Him, too.

> I believe in God the Father almighty, Creator of heaven and earth.

And right away the Creed affirms the Incarnation of our Lord:

> And in Jesus Christ His only Son our Lord; Who was conceived by the Holy Ghost, born of the Virgin Mary, suffered under Pontius Pilate, was crucified, died and was buried. He descended into hell, the third day He rose again from the dead; He ascended into heaven, sitteth at the right hand of God the Father almighty, from thence He shall come to judge the living and the dead.

Everything that is said of the Holy Ghost also applies to our Lord because it is His Spirit, and He announced to the apostles that He would send them His Spirit, the Spirit that proceeds from Him.

> I believe in the Holy Ghost, the Holy Catholic Church (which He founded), the Communion of saints, the forgiveness of sins, the resurrection of the body and life everlasting. Amen.

Notice in this text the importance given to the life of our Lord, and especially to His Passion. God wanted to realize His Incarnation and His work by means of His life in Palestine, thus by His hidden life of thirty years, and then by His public life, His Passion, His death, Resurrection and Ascension. All of this was willed from all eternity by God, thus willed by Himself because Jesus is God.

We must love to think over the whole life of our Lord in order better to grasp the great mystery which is our Lord and which unites in Him the three grand mysteries of the Trinity, the Incarnation, and the Redemption. The *Creed* is a nourishing spiritual food. There is no need to look for a difficult and complicated topic for our meditation; the *Creed* offers us a very fruitful one, and initiates us into the great mysteries which are to be our consolation here below and our joy in heaven.

The Symbol of Nicea is even more explicit:

> I believe in one God, the Father almighty, Maker of heaven and earth, and of all things, visible and invisible. And in one Lord Jesus Christ, the only begotten Son of God. And born of the Father, before all ages. God of God: Light of Light: true God of true God. Begotten, not made, consubstantial with the Father...

Here it is a question of the Divine nature of our Lord, by whom all things were made. Then comes His Incarnation:

> Who, for us men, and for our salvation, came down from heaven. And became incarnate by the Holy Ghost of the Virgin Mary: and was made man. He was crucified also for us,

> suffered under Pontius Pilate, and was buried. And the third day He rose again according to the Scriptures. And ascended into heaven, and sitteth at the right hand of the Father. And he shall come again with glory to judge both the living and the dead, of whose kingdom there shall be no end....

All the clauses of these sentences take on considerable importance. The *Credo* is short, quickly read or recited, but it is the very thing that men should know and meditate all their life long. After all, knowing what God has done for us is the most essential thing.

It is clearly affirmed that God is the Creator of all things: our Lord who is God is our Creator. He is the Word of God by whom all was made, hence He is both our Beginning and our End. He desired to make Himself our way which leads to the end; and not only our way, but also our nourishment, and also to be our brother and to communicate to us the divine life. It is an admirable history. Our Lord is the measure of the worth of persons and things. To the degree that the one and the other are nearer our Lord they have real worth, true worth. Clearly, then, it is the most Blessed Virgin and St. Joseph who hold the first places.

In spirituality, there is a tendency to minimize the place and the role of St. Joseph; yet he held an extraordinary place in the economy of the Incarnation and the Redemption. To him were confided the Mother of Jesus, and Jesus himself, thus God Himself. He certainly received very special graces of light on the mystery of the Incarnation.

In the measure that men are close to our Lord, they become transformed in our Lord, they live in our Lord. This is seen in the history of the Church: it is around our Lord that families, communities, villages and towns are constituted. Literally, all live around our Lord. Even professional associations had their patron saints and feastdays within the profession, within society. In the family, the entire atmosphere was imbued with the presence of our Lord. We must try to restore this ambiance, and introduce the presence of our Lord once again into our daily lives, and His royalty into the course of everyday public life. We must become truly Christian once again.

We must dwell upon the mystery of our Lord Jesus Christ, and believe in His Divinity, for He is God.

The Nicene Creed continues:

> I believe in the Holy Spirit, the Lord, the giver of life, who proceeds from the Father and the Son. Together with the Father and the Son he is adored and glorified; he it was who spoke through the prophets.
>
> I believe in one, holy, catholic, and apostolic church. I profess one baptism for the remission of sins. And I look forward to the resurrection of the dead, and the life of the world to come. Amen.

Notice that the Symbol of Nicea begins with this sentence: "I believe in one God"; hence, there are not several Gods. When the highest authority of the Church and the bishops go so far as to say: "We have the same God," in speaking of the Moslems, it is incredible. For they do not believe in the Blessed Trinity, and they do not have the same Faith as we do. The god they adore will give them, so they think, a hundredfold of the material goods they enjoy on earth. The richer one is, the richer one will be; the more concubines one has, the more one will have in the figment they paint for themselves of heaven....Such is the god of the Moslems, whom we are told is He whom we adore!

Such statements are senseless and blasphemous.

CHAPTER 5

THE LOVE SONG OF GOD

Let us also reread the magnificent Symbol of St. Athanasius which used to be recited in the breviary every Sunday at the hour of Prime:

> Whosoever will be saved, before all things it is necessary that he hold the Catholic Faith. Which Faith except everyone do keep whole and undefiled, without doubt he shall perish everlastingly.

Without the Catholic Faith, one cannot be saved. It is clear. But go and tell this now!...

> And the Catholic Faith is this, that we worship one God in Trinity and Trinity in Unity. Neither confounding the Persons, nor dividing the Substance. For there is one Person of the Father, another of the Son, and another of the Holy Ghost. But the Godhead of the Father, of the Son and of the Holy Ghost is all One, the Glory Equal, the Majesty Co-Eternal. Such as the Father is, such is the Son, and such is the Holy Ghost. The Father Uncreate, the Son Uncreate, and the Holy Ghost Uncreate. The Father Incomprehensible, the Son Incomprehensible, and the Holy Ghost Incomprehensible. The Father Eternal, the Son Eternal, and the Holy Ghost Eternal, and yet they are not Three Eternals but One Eternal. As also there are not Three Uncreated, nor Three Incomprehensibles, but One Uncreated, and One Incomprehensible. So likewise the Father is Almighty, the Son Almighty, and the Holy Ghost Almighty. And yet they are not Three Almighties but One Almighty.

By its terseness, preciseness and clarity, this formulation of our Faith compels our admiration.

> So the Father is God, the Son is God, and the Holy Ghost is God. And yet they are not Three Gods, but One God. So likewise the Father is Lord, the Son Lord, and the Holy Ghost Lord. And yet not Three Lords but One Lord. For, like as we are compelled by the Christian verity to acknowledge every

> Person by Himself to be God and Lord, so are we forbidden by the Catholic Religion to say, there be Three Gods or Three Lords. The Father is made of none, neither created, nor begotten. The Son is of the Father alone; not made, nor created, but begotten. The Holy Ghost is of the Father, and of the Son: neither made, nor created, nor begotten, but proceeding.

The terms chosen by St. Athanasius are perfectly clear and express the truths of our Faith, it can be said, definitively. This *Credo* cannot be changed. No alteration is possible. Its expressions, which have been thus used and confirmed by the Holy Church, cannot be accommodated to interpretations which would modify their meaning. But the modernists and modern theologians cannot abide this. They no longer wish to admit that the formulas of our Faith are definitive. According to them, the Faith must always be expressed in relation to the evolution of modern times, according to the times in which we are living.

If it were necessary to utilize other terms to express these same truths, under pretext of choosing words or definitions better adapted to modern philosophy or the modern mind or the science of our times, what could we look for? These would be terms and definitions that would lose the exact meaning that the old formulas have always had and which have been explained for centuries by theologians to express exactly the content of the Catholic Faith. It is impossible to introduce such changes.

> So there is One Father, not Three Fathers; one Son, not Three Sons; One Holy Ghost, not Three Holy Ghosts. And in this Trinity none is afore or after Other, None is greater or less than Another, but the whole Three Persons are Co-eternal together, and Co-equal.
>
> So that in all things, as is aforesaid, the Unity in Trinity, and the Trinity in Unity is to be worshipped. He therefore that will be saved, must thus think of the Trinity.

Now that is clear and precise.

> Furthermore, it is necessary to everlasting Salvation, that he

> also believe rightly the Incarnation of our Lord Jesus Christ. For the right Faith is, that we believe and confess, that our Lord Jesus Christ, the Son of God, is God and Man. God, of the substance of the Father, Begotten before the worlds; and Man, of the substance of His mother, born into the world. Perfect God and Perfect Man, of a reasonable Soul and human Flesh subsisting. Equal to the Father as touching His Godhead, and inferior to the Father as touching His Manhood.

This statement of our Faith is admirable, and with great clarity it annihilates all the heresies concerning the divinity of our Lord Jesus Christ made Man.

> Who, although He be God and Man, yet He is not two, but One Christ. One, not by conversion of the Godhead into Flesh, but by taking of the Manhood into God. One altogether, not by confusion of substance, but by Unity of Person. For as the reasonable soul and flesh is one Man, so God and Man is one Christ. Who suffered for our salvation, descended into Hell, rose again the third day from the dead. He ascended into Heaven, He sitteth on the right hand of the Father, God Almighty, from which he shall come to judge the quick and the dead. At whose coming all men shall rise again with their bodies, and shall give account for their own works. And they that have done good shall go into life everlasting, and they that have done evil into everlasting fire. This is the Catholic Faith, which except a man believe faithfully and firmly, he cannot be saved.

It is very important, then, to know well what these three Symbols express and to live accordingly. Each time we recite the Creed or sing the *Credo*, let us make a deliberate effort to be truly conscious of the fact that the words we pronounce constitute the summary of all that we must believe and love. It is the deepest and dearest reality of our pilgrimage in time, because it expresses all that our Lord, that is, all that God has done to love us. It is the song of love of the good God for us. That is what the *Credo* really is: the résumé of the charity of God for us. It is magnificent.

Sic nos amentem quis non redamaret, sings the sacred liturgy in the *Adeste Fideles* of Christmas, following the thought of St. Augustine: "How can we fail to love in return someone who has so loved us?"

Each time we recite or sing the *Credo*, let us remember this appeal to our love, to the charity that we should have towards God. Let us strive to be mindful of this appeal to orient ourselves ever more closely so as to love God truly, to thank Him, to offer thanksgiving, and to do everything in our power to assure that His love for us be not in vain.

It is terrible to realize that all that our Lord did, that all God does for us, might be futile, and that there might not be any response to this love. Then we understand that the justice of God permits and wills that those who refuse this love be deprived of it for all eternity. It is a frightening consideration, about which God Himself can do nothing, for it is man himself who closes the way to the love of God in him, who refuses to recognize our Lord Jesus Christ, God Creator of all things, who shuts himself up in his egocentrism and pride, refusing all light.

As St. John wrote: "And the light shineth in darkness: and the darkness did not comprehend it" (Jn. 1:5). God came to His own family, and His own rejected Him, except those to whom the good God has given the grace to be children of God (*cf.* Jn. 1:11-12).

CHAPTER 6

JESUS CHRIST, ETERNAL WISDOM

Where else besides Holy Scripture and the acts of the magisterium of the Church can we find that most consoling and encouraging affirmation of the divinity of our Lord, of His life and His love for us? In the liturgy, for the whole liturgy sings to us of our Lord Jesus Christ; it sings of the love of God for us by every means and modality.

And it is for this very reason, that is, because the divinity of our Lord is sung in the liturgy, because His royalty is manifested there at every instant by word, action, and adoration, that the liturgy now must disappear. For the enemies of our Lord no longer wish to hear His royalty spoken of publicly in society. Instead, the liturgy has become the public act of praise rendered to humanity, to man himself. The public homage given to the royalty of our Lord and to His divinity has become intolerable to them.

Since we are now being told that the Moslems and Jews adore the same God as we Catholics, it is not without interest to be acquainted with a passage from a book titled *Portrait of a Jew*, published in 1962 by Albert Memmi, a Jew of Tunisian origin who, after being expelled from Tunisia, settled in France:

> Are the Christians really aware of what the name of Jesus, their God, means to a Jew?...For a Jew who has not ceased to believe and practice his own religion, Christianity is the greatest theological and metaphysical usurpation of history; it is a blasphemy, a spiritual scandal, and an act of subversion. For all Jews, even atheists, the name of Jesus is the symbol of a threat, a heavy menace that has been hanging over their heads for centuries, and which is always threatening to explode into catastrophe without their knowing why or how to parry. This

> name is part of an absurd, delirious accusation which despite being groundless nevertheless is of such an efficacious cruelty that it makes their life in society nearly unbearable. This name has come to be one of the signs, one of the names of the immense system that surrounds, condemns and excludes them. May my Christian friends pardon me; so that they can better understand me, and to adopt their own language, I will say that for the Jews, their God is a bit like the devil, if the devil, as they claim, is the symbol and the essence of evil on earth, iniquitous and all powerful, incomprehensible and resolved to crush the hapless humans....

This is what a Jew thinks of our Lord Jesus Christ. One must not delude oneself; we are faced with people who bear the hatred of Jesus in their hearts. And if the adversaries of our Lord Jesus Christ feel real hatred for Him, a diabolical hatred, we Christians, on the contrary, should actively desire that He become the center of our thoughts, our affections, our souls, and all our activity.

St. Louis Grignion de Montfort utilized a language both simple and profound to express this thought in *The Love of Eternal Wisdom*:

> Is it possible for man to love that which he does not know? Can he love ardently that which he knows but imperfectly? Why then is the adorable Jesus, Eternal and Incarnate Wisdom, loved so little? Because He is not known, or known but little. Very few of us, like St. Paul, make a sincere study of the supereminent science of Jesus which is nevertheless the most noble, the most consoling, the most useful and the most necessary of all sciences in heaven and on earth.[11]

And he continues:

> St. John Chrysostom tells us that our Lord is a summary of all the works of God; an epitome of all God's perfections and of all the perfections of His creatures, in these words: "Jesus Christ, eternal Wisdom, is all that you can and should wish for. Long for Him, seek Him; He is the most precious pearl you should wish to acquire even at the cost of selling all that you

---

[11] St. Louis de Montfort, *Love of Eternal Wisdom*. Rev. Ed. Bayshore, NY: Montfort Publications, 1960. Ch. 1, no. 8.

> possess."[12] ...Nothing is more consoling than to know Divine Wisdom. Blessed are they who listen to Him; more blessed still they who long for Him and seek after Him. Blessed above all are they who teach His ways, who experience within their hearts the intimate sweetness of Him Who is at once the joy and happiness of the eternal Father and the glory of the Angels.[13]
>
> This knowledge of Eternal wisdom is not only the most noble and consoling, it is also the most useful and the most necessary, because "Eternal Life is to know God and His Son Jesus Christ" (Jn. 17:3)....If we really wish to obtain life everlasting, let us acquire knowledge of Divine Wisdom...[14]

Then St. Louis de Montfort summarizes in a few words these sentences which are already to be found in the writings of the Fathers of the Church:

> To know Jesus Christ, Eternal Wisdom, is to know enough; to know everything and not to know Him, is to know nothing.[15]

Who knows Christ knows enough, even if he knows nothing else; who does not know Christ knows nothing, even if he knows everything else.

We should often repeat and meditate on these words. Those who have never studied who and what our Lord is, the wise men of this world who scarcely know Him, find this assertion very difficult to admit. They cannot understand because they do not have the Faith. It is faith which teaches us that everything is in our Lord Jesus Christ. Why is everything in our Lord Jesus Christ? Because our Lord is God, and everything is in God. The reply is simple and accessible, even if it seems difficult to some to admit that this man was God. St. Louis de Montfort continues:

> What does it avail an archer to know how to hit the outer

---

12 (*Ibid.*, no. 9).
13 *Ibid.*, no. 10.
14 *Ibid.*, no. 11.
15 *Ibid.*

> parts of the target, if he does not know how to hit the center? What will it avail us to know all other sciences necessary for salvation, if we do not know the only essential one, the center to which all others must converge, Jesus Christ?[16]

St. Paul, as sure of himself as he was and so well versed in classical letters, nonetheless said:

> For I judged not myself to know anything among you, but Jesus Christ: and him crucified (I Cor. 2:2).

This is the résumé of our faith, and what deeply interests men, despite what one may think or say about it. Even though our civilization is becoming less and less Christian, most of us still live in social circles accustomed to these Christian truths. Yet we are no longer adequately aware of what our Lord Jesus Christ gave to our society and our families. We find it natural. Of course, we are disappointed to see that little by little holiness is disappearing from home and hearth, and Catholic order from public life.

To really measure all that our Lord brought to our society, perhaps it is necessary to have been in contact with pagan peoples. Of the thirteen years I was in Gabon, seven of them were spent in the bush. I had therefore the opportunity to speak to these pagans in their own language and to teach them the Gospel and thereby enable them to discover our Lord Jesus Christ, and approach Him. It is impossible to imagine the impact made upon these absolutely uncultivated souls, knowing neither how to read nor write, when one spoke to them about our Lord Jesus Christ and about the Cross of our Lord. It is just what St. Paul said: it was what they needed and were waiting for.

Similarly, while visiting the oases in the Sahara, I had contacts with the Moslem peoples. I went into the schools of the Holy Ghost Fathers and Sisters. What interested the children? It was hearing about religion, about our Lord

---

16 *Ibid.*, no. 12.

Jesus Christ. As soon as one turned to other subjects, their minds wandered; as long as one spoke to them about religion, their little eyes opened wide and they were attentive.

This might at first glance seem surprising; and yet, it is not at all. Rather, it is very natural. Our Lord is their God, their Creator, and it is impossible for there not to be an affinity between the One who created and redeemed them, and themselves, between their Creator and their souls; and, consequently, the simple fact of speaking of our Lord to these souls captivated them.

About fifteen years before the Council, progressive catechisms were drawn up under the pretext that one must not teach the truths of the Faith to children because they cannot understand them; that one must first teach them natural truths, prove to them the existence of God, and then very gently lead them to religious truth. Only when they have understood about the existence of God might one begin to speak to them about revelation and Jesus Christ. What an aberration! Utter madness! For one forgets that our Lord Jesus Christ is also the Creator. On the contrary, nothing is more likely to transform souls, even those of children, than to speak to them about our Lord Jesus Christ, and to recount His life. It is a very grave error to believe that it is necessary to wait to speak to children about our Lord Jesus Christ until they know the truths of natural religion.

There are also those who affirm, and this occurs frequently, that in the missions, the missionaries should not preach religion to the infidels until they have given them a minimal standard of living. Of what use is it, they argue, to preach the Gospel to people who live in a completely deficient social, and even physical, environment. But this reasoning is absurd and, let us add, truly almost diabolical, because it means depriving these people and these children of that which is most precious and beautiful for them, and which they are quite capable of receiving. Ultimately, it means depriving them of the very thing they are most capable of adapting themselves to, even more rapidly and more easily, perhaps, than can those persons who are well endowed and live comfortably.

In her admirable *Magnificat*, the Blessed Virgin Mary says:

> *Esurientes implevit bonis, et divites dimisit inanes* (Lk. 1:53). He hath filled the hungry with good things, and the rich He hath sent empty away.

So, they would like to make these poor people who are ready and able to receive the truth of our Lord rich according to the world's standard, and deprive them of what brings true happiness; for it is not from riches that a truly happy life springs.

When teaching them the Gospel and the Faith, one could see these tribes become Christian, become transformed. One could almost tell by reading their faces which were Christian and which were not. The faces of the Christians were serene, radiating peace, while the others were often contracted by fear, subject to a kind of perpetual dread of the spirits surrounding them, always ready to do them evil. Their faces certainly did not reflect happiness. The face of the Christian who is delivered from these pagan beliefs and who places his hope in God, who rests in God, is relaxed, cheerful and peaceful.

These few reflections are brought forth to refute the false principles according to which one would refrain from giving our Lord Jesus Christ to those who seek Him, need Him, and are waiting for Him. It is not charitable to say that first of all it is necessary to give these poor peoples a more humane standard of living, after which one will preach to them the Gospel. True charity consists in giving them straight away what is essential, that is the foundation of their joy, their happiness, and their interior transformation.

It is false to affirm that to preach the Gospel is simply to incite people to endure patiently insults and trials, without giving them joy and without trying to diminish injustices. It is by preaching our Lord Jesus Christ that injustices will disappear. To the degree that people believe in our Lord Jesus Christ and are subject to Him, and hence to His law of love, they will acquire the concern to practice charity and to give everyone his due. The immediate consequence will be that humane relationships and justice will be re-established. This is the only way, there is no other, for our Lord is the source of all good. It is not by class struggle that justice can be re-established, but by preaching the reign of our Lord Jesus Christ. There is no greater service one can render to souls in order to lead them to their salvation. There is no greater source of social and civic well-being or of familial integrity than our Lord Jesus Christ. Good Christians found good Christian families who know how to bear their trials and give mutual support. By maintaining a Christian home, they obey the law of God.

Nowadays, they seek means and methods for increasing the standard of living, and only this counts. But when all is said and done, one still notices that the same injustices continue more or less because they have repudiated the law of our Lord Jesus Christ. Big financial scandals and injustices erupt because people have lost the notions of charity and of justice.

Let us not listen to these false prophets who would keep us from speaking of our Lord and oblige us to find another means to please men and save them. All that is false.

Taking inspiration from the Epistle of St. Paul to the Philippians (3:7-8), St. Louis de Montfort expresses his choice:

> I now see and appreciate that this knowledge is so excellent, so delightful, so profitable and so admirable that I take no account of all that pleased me before. All else is void of meaning, absurd and a waste of time.[17]

Commenting on another passage of St. Paul (Col. 2:4-8), St. Grignion de Montfort continues:

> I say to you that Jesus Christ is the abyss of all knowledge, that you may neither be deceived by the specious or high-sounding words of orators nor by the deceptive subtleties of philosophers. "Grow in grace and in the knowledge of our Lord and Savior Jesus Christ" (II Pet. 3:18).[18]

In this work, *The Love of Eternal Wisdom*, in speaking of the Word Incarnate who is Eternal Wisdom, he tells us how to approach Him, know and imitate Him. The shortest way to arrive at the goal is the Blessed Virgin Mary, for she is the way that leads us to perfection. Such was the spirituality of St. Louis de Montfort. His first devotion was directed to Eternal Wisdom, to our Lord Jesus Christ, as he wrote:

> Christ is our doctrine, it is He who teaches us. Christ is our Master, it is from Him that we learn. Christ is our school, in Him we learn. Because Christ is the one and only messenger, the light on all questions, He has the key to all human problems. Our world must relearn to know the One to whom it owes all that it is. It is necessary to speak to it of our Lord Jesus Christ over and over without tiring. If the world knows Him in His doctrine and His works, it will rediscover in Him the Lord and Master whom false guides and unworthy pastors have made it forget. And so helped to return to the source of all goods, it will find once again the Way, the Truth, and the Life. [Source of citation not identified.]

---

[17] *Ibid.*, no. 12.
[18] *Ibid.*

CHAPTER 6

THE LITURGY: JESUS CHRIST COMMUNICATED

We have examined the professions of faith of the Church, the attitude of the Church's enemies towards our Lord and the manifestations of His divinity. Now let's look at the place that our Lord holds in the liturgy and in the life of the Church. It is in the liturgy that the Church expresses most perfectly what she thinks of our Lord Jesus Christ and what she asks us to contemplate in His Person. It would be wrong to think of the liturgy as just a beautiful page of history that is recounted to us throughout the year. To consider the liturgy under this aspect alone would be to misunderstand it.

The liturgy is not just a reminder of the events of the life of our Lord, of His actions and His teaching; it is above all a life. By means of the liturgy, our Lord communicates to us not only the Faith, but also sanctification. He communicates to us His grace, sanctifying grace. For the Church, it is clear that the central point of the salutary action that communicates grace to us is the holy sacrifice of the Mass. In order to help us participate more fully in the Mass, the Church has set it amidst a cycle of feasts and reminders of the life of our Lord and the lives of the saints. Each event of the life of our Lord brings a particular grace. Unfortunately, left to ourselves we are unable to understand the depth and magnitude of the mystery of our Lord. That is why the Church, like a wise mother, adapts it to our level. She distributes the graces of the liturgy throughout the year marked by the feasts of our Lord, and especially by the two great cycles of the liturgical year, Christmas and Easter.

This is what Fr. Pius Parsch in *Guide to the Liturgical Year* expresses:

> What should we expect of the liturgical year? Divine life, and life in abundance. The divine life planted in our soul by the sacrament of Baptism must develop during the ecclesiastical year, and tend to its perfection by means of liturgical prayer. The liturgy is like a precious ring whose diamond is the Eucharist and the eucharistic Sacrifice, and whose setting is formed by the feasts and the ecclesiastical seasons.
>
> The journey through the liturgical year is like an excursion in the mountains. There are two peaks to climb: the first summit which is the mountain of Christmas, and the dominant peak which is the mountain of Easter. In both cases there is an ascent, the time of preparation: Advent before Christmas, Lent before Easter; and a walk along the ridge from one peak to another, from Christmas till Epiphany, and from Easter to Pentecost.

This image given us by Fr. Parsch helps us to understand better what the liturgical year is:

> Consequently, we have two cycles of feasts to travel through. In both, the object of their particular considerations is the kingdom of God in the soul and in the Church. Twice a year we seek the kingdom of God, we find it, and we build it. In the ecclesiastical year, the Church teaches us. It is a school of the Faith.
>
> Throughout the course of the liturgical year, the truths of the Faith, one by one, are presented and recalled to us. The liturgical year is a zealous educator; it desires not only to communicate to us the truths of the Faith, but it wants to make us better and bring us up for heaven. Every day of the liturgical year the same appeal is addressed to our hearts: "Take off the old man and put on the new."

This is what Dom Gaspard Lefebvre also reminds us. It must be remembered that from the beginning of the century, a considerable effort was made to enable the faithful to better understand the liturgy. And the faithful were very interested. *The Liturgical Year* by Dom Guéranger, for example, was extraordinarily successful. It used to be that one could easily find people who assisted at Mass with a book of *The Liturgical Year* in hand. Or at least many people had it in their library, and loved to prepare themselves for the Mass by reading from its pages.

If we really desire to penetrate the mystery of our Lord, to know Him truly, to love Him as we ought to love Him, to cleave to Him and to receive His graces, it is absolutely necessary to know, study, and appreciate the liturgy. This is certainly a great means of sanctification:

> Public worship, rites, sacraments, official prayers, feast days and liturgical seasons are all means which the Church uses to unite us to Christ and to transform our souls unto His own likeness. Each year from Advent to Pentecost, she has us celebrate the principal events of the life of the Savior, not as a mere reminder....

Which is the opinion of the Protestants. For them, the liturgy (if indeed the liturgy can be modified by the adjective Protestant) is only a reminder, a history that is narrated about the life of our Lord. It lacks the vital significance it has for Catholics, and it is not the source of life and sanctification which is capital for all Catholics. Our Lord desired that His life, the life of grace, be transmitted by means of the sacraments and by the liturgy:

> ....but to renew us by the application of the particular graces that He brings us at each celebration. The vital communication of the mysteries of Christ imbues our souls with an authentic Christian life intimately tied to the life of the Church. The meaning and the spirit of these liturgical celebrations is impressed upon us by the Church herself. One has only to let oneself be guided by her in order to reach the heart of the Christian mystery and to profit fully from its supernatural efficacy.

Dom Marmion says the same in an admirable way:

> Guided by the Holy Spirit, Who is the Spirit of Jesus Him-

> self, the Church unfolds every year before the eyes of her children, from Christmas to the Ascension, the complete cycle of the mysteries of Christ, sometimes greatly condensed, sometimes in their strict chronological order, as during Holy Week and Eastertide. She thus makes us relive, by a very animated and lively representation, each of the mysteries of her Divine Spouse; she makes us retrace each of the stages of His life. If we allow ourselves to be conducted by her, infallibly we shall end by knowing the mysteries of Jesus and especially we shall penetrate the sentiments of His divine heart. (*Christ in His Mysteries*, p.22; French ed.).

It is in fact because the mysteries of Christ, Dom Marmion says, are not just scenes to look upon and examples to imitate; they are also sources of graces. There is thus a special grace attached to each mystery of our Lord in the liturgy: spiritual rebirth (Christmas), death to sin (the Passion), freedom of soul and living for God (Easter), life in heaven by faith (the Ascension):

> By following Christ Jesus in all His mysteries in this way, by uniting ourselves to Him, little by little yet surely, and each time more intensely, we shall participate in His divinity, in His divine life. According to the beautiful sentence of St. Augustine: "What came to pass before in a divine reality, is renewed spiritually in pious souls by the repeated celebration of these mysteries"[19] (*Op. cit.*, pp.26–27).

[19] "*Quod semel factum in rebus veritas indicat, hoc saepius celebrandum in cordibus piis solemnitas renovat*" (Sermo 220, in vigil. Paschae II).

CHAPTER 8

PER DOMINUM NOSTRUM JESUM CHRISTUM

In addition to the Common of the Mass, the Church has composed the propers, which always contain a lesson related to the day's feast. These prayers, very short yet so beautiful, offer us on every occasion a thought-provoking subject of meditation. One is surprised to notice the profundity with which the Church has thought out these prayers, thus putting at our disposition each day a truth of the Faith. One marvels at the richness of the liturgy, whether considering the Introits or the Graduals. What profound and moving thoughts are found there: appeals to the mercy and goodness of God, to His praise!

In all these prayers one always finds the four ends of the holy sacrifice of the Mass. The first end is the offering of latria, the worship of adoration and praise due to God alone. The second, the eucharistic end, is thanksgiving, the giving of thanks for all the graces with which the good Lord blesses us. Then comes the propitiatory or expiatory end, which from the Catholic point of view is essential. It is this end that is denied by the Protestants. They refuse to believe that the sacrifice of the Mass is really an expiatory sacrifice. At the limit they will grant that it is a sacrifice of thanksgiving. They do not deny the expression, but they absolutely deny the character of "expiatory sacrifice." They claim that everything was accomplished at Calvary, and there is nothing more to do afterwards. There is no individual application of the sacrifice, except by an interior sentiment of confidence in God.

The faith of Protestants is not at all the faith of Catholics. It consists in a natural sentiment of confidence in God. It is not the adherence of the intelligence to revealed truths because of the authority of God who reveals them. Yet such is the definition of Catholic faith: it is the submission of our understanding to objective truths that are given to us by divine revelation. For the Protestants, it is merely a sentiment of confidence in our Lord. One need not be worried about one's salvation, it will come of itself. And so they reject the propitiatory end of sacrifice.

In the new Mass, all the texts that had the purpose of affirming in a very clear and precise manner the propitiatory end of the holy sacrifice of the Mass were erased. Only one or two allusions remain.

Lastly, the fourth end of sacrifice is petition, that is, the expression of the different requests we address to God for our spiritual welfare and that of our neighbor, and even for the temporal graces that we need.

These four ends of the holy sacrifice of the Mass are essential for Catholics: latria, thanksgiving, propitiation and petition. And one notices that all the texts of the liturgy, all of them, can be assigned to one or the other of these four ends. Sometimes adoration predominates, sometimes thanksgiving, sometimes it is the admission of our sins and miseries and an appeal to the mercy of the good Lord, and then finally the request for the goods that we need. All of this is accomplished with such an art and with such a maternal concern of the Church to awaken in our hearts the same sentiments towards our Lord, that the liturgy is truly a wonder.

We have seen the solicitude of Dom Guéranger to preserve, by all he did, the extraordinary source of graces which is the liturgy, the fundamental source of the life of the Church.[20] With all the deviations which, alas! have been introduced everywhere, the faithful no longer receive the graces which they have a right to and which they need.

Throughout the liturgy, the conclusion of our prayers is always: "By our Lord Jesus Christ," "With our Lord Jesus Christ," "In our Lord Jesus Christ...."[21] The Church avoids giving a purely theistic religion in which our Lord would not intervene. For her, our Lord is All. He is her mystical Spouse and the Church never forgets it. She always prays *per Christum Dominum nostrum*, "by our Lord Jesus Christ." There is no question of obtaining any grace without Him.

In the new Canon of the Mass, they suppressed "*per Christum Dominum nostrum*"! How was such a thing possible? By what aberration or malignity were the reformers able to erase these words at the end of the prayers of the Canon? One really wonders. On the contrary, the Church makes a point of insisting that every grace comes to us by our Lord; all must return to God by our Lord. He is truly the Mediator. There is no other. We are obliged to go by way of Him whether to receive or to give, if we have anything we can give to God: our praises, our oblation, our thanks. This is only possible through our Lord Jesus Christ.

And this is how our faith is continually deepened, by the insistence of the Church on the mediation of our Lord Jesus Christ. He is our only Savior. He is our salvation. This is the major, the essential truth of faith.

Were we to put our Lord Jesus Christ to the side, our life would no longer have any meaning. And this applies not only to our personal spiritual life, our interior life, but also to our whole life, professional, familial, civic. The life

---

[20] "First and indispensable source of the true Christian spirit," says St. Pius X in his *motu proprio* of November 23, 1903.

[21] Except during Advent, when the Church is awaiting her Mediator, and on a few other occasions.

of men has no more meaning if Jesus Christ is put aside. The liturgy justly accustoms us to ask for everything through our Lord Jesus Christ, even for the blessings and temporal goods we need in the city.

After having expressed the importance that our Lord Jesus Christ must have in our life, and after the affirmations of the Church concerning His divinity, the liturgy shows us our Lord as the center, the object and the end of our prayers.

It used to be that when in Rome one felt these convictions. Rome was truly a school of the Faith, just as the liturgy is a school of the Faith. More than fifty years ago, this city exuded faith in our Lord. In St. Peter's Basilica, where I had the joy of attending the canonizations of St. Theresa of the Child Jesus and of the Curé of Ars, it really felt like no longer being on this earth. Everything respired faith in our Lord, faith in God, in the Holy Trinity. It was really the living Church singing the praises of God, magnifying our Lord Jesus Christ in His saints. Someone staying at Rome who failed to increase the intensity, firmness and fervor of his Catholic faith would have understood nothing of the city of Rome in which he was living.

Now, unfortunately, that has changed; diplomatic questions and human problems have taken precedence over matters of faith. It is an immense pity for the Church and the faithful, but now the Church lives according to this all too human manner. She isn't dead. She cannot die. The true face of the Church still remains in the Rome that keeps the faith, even if it is no longer as apparent as it used to be. In Rome, the Church may really descend into the catacombs, but the Church, after all, is not just Rome, it is also all those who are attached to our Lord, who serve Him, who live by Him and who belong to the Mystical Body of our Lord Jesus Christ.

Our Lord is a veritable reality: He lives, He must live; He must reign, everyone must be at His service so that His reign come. And for this, it is necessary to have a profound faith in our Lord, especially in His divinity.

CHAPTER 9

ONE OF THE BLESSED TRINITY

The life of faith depends upon our profound belief in the divinity of our Lord. To really grasp that our Lord Jesus Christ is God, it is helpful to consider His interior life, and doing so, we encounter there the Holy Trinity. Our Lord possessed the beatific vision in His human soul, and so lived by the glory of the Blessed Trinity. And as He was Himself God, the Son of God, all the more did He live, by His divine nature, of the life of the Holy Trinity. The interior life of the Blessed Trinity is the first of our dogmas, it is the basis and the essential dogma of our faith. It is impossible to be a Catholic if one does not believe in our Lord or in the Blessed Trinity. For who is our Lord, if not one of the Persons of the Blessed Trinity. We cannot believe in our Lord without believing in the Blessed Trinity; equally, to not believe in the Blessed Trinity is to not believe in our Lord. All of this is intimately connected. Certainly, it is an unfathomable mystery. Nevertheless we can try to understand this mystery a little, as much as our Lord has revealed it to us, not by reason, but by faith.

The Catechism of the Council of Trent gives a brief summary of what the Faith teaches us on this subject. We believe that our Lord is truly the Son of God, and that He is one of the Persons of the Blessed Trinity, consubstantially united to the Father and the Holy Ghost, and that He thus possesses all the attributes of God, all the privileges of God because He is God: this aspect shows our Lord Jesus Christ in His true stature. Do not see in our Lord Jesus Christ just His humanity. Certainly, it is easier to imagine our Lord as the Man He was: a child at Bethlehem and Nazareth, and then the man preaching in Palestine and crucified on the cross. We can and we must imagine Him thus. St. Thomas Aquinas says that our prayer cannot separate us from our Lord Jesus Christ if we consider Him in His humanity, because the humanity of our Lord necessarily leads us to His divinity. While we must purify our minds of worldly images that could distract us in our prayer, the humanity of our Lord can never be a distraction because it is intimately united to His divinity.

We must constantly remind ourselves that this humanity cloaks the divinity, and that it is a miracle that our Lord was not always radiant as when He appeared on Mount Tabor during the Transfiguration. Normally He should have been radiant and have had a glorious body because He enjoyed the beatific vision. But in order to die for us on the cross and to suffer for us, our Lord wanted to really wed our mortal condition such as it is, capable of suffering and death.

Speaking of the Apostles' Creed, the Catechism of the Council of Trent says:

> This name [of Father] implies that in the one Essence of the Godhead is proposed to our belief, not only one Person, but a distinction of persons; for in one Divine Nature there are Three Persons—the Father, begotten of none; the Son, begotten of the Father before all ages; the Holy Ghost, proceeding from the Father and the Son, likewise, from all eternity. In the one Substance of the Divinity the Father is the First Person, who with His Only-begotten Son, and the Holy Ghost, is one God and one Lord, not in the singularity of one Person, but in the trinity of one Substance.[22]

---

22 *The Catechism of the Council of Trent.* McHugh, John A., O.P., and Callan, Charles J., O.P., tr. Rockford, IL: TAN Books & Publishers, 1982. pp.21-22.

That is why one can say in all truth that we have only one God, our Lord Jesus Christ; because our Lord is God the Son, and because God the Son is never apart from God the Father and God the Holy Ghost with whom He makes one God. What we believe of God, we must proclaim the same of our Lord Jesus Christ: *Tu solus sanctus, tu solus Dominus, tu solus Altissimus, Jesu Christe.* You alone are our Lord. And this is what St. Paul says in the epistle to the Ephesians (4:5): *Unus Dominus, una fides, unum baptisma,* One Lord, one faith, one baptism.

We do not have two or three Lords because we have only one Lord; we do not have two or three Gods, we have only one God: our Lord Jesus Christ, that is to say, God the Son with the Father and the Holy Ghost. It is a mystery, the mystery of our Lord Jesus Christ.

This mystery is for us also a source of consolation, because when we receive our Lord Jesus Christ in us by Holy Communion, we must know that we receive our Lord, and consequently the three Persons. In fact, our Lord cannot separate Himself from the other two Persons. He is the Son of God consubstantially and essentially united to the others. He is inseparable from the other Persons.

The Council of Trent makes this clear:

> These Three Persons, since it would be impiety to assert that they are unlike or unequal in any thing, are understood to be distinct only in their respective properties. For the Father is unbegotten, the Son begotten of the Father, and the Holy Ghost proceeds from both. Thus we acknowledge the Essence and the Substance of the Three Persons to be the same in such wise that we believe that in confessing the true and eternal God we are piously and religiously to adore distinction in the Persons, unity in the Essence, and equality in the Trinity.
>
> Hence, when we say that the Father is the First Person, we are not to be understood to mean that in the Trinity there is anything first or last, greater or less. Let none of the faithful be guilty of such impiety, for the Christian religion proclaims the

> same eternity, the same majesty of glory in the Three Persons. But since the Father is the Beginning without a beginning, we truly and unhesitatingly affirm that He is the First Person....[23]

Evidently, when we say First Person, we immediately have the feeling that the Father existed first because there was the Son and the Holy Ghost. But there never was a moment, not even a thousandth of a second, when the Father would have existed without the Son and the Holy Ghost. They have always existed consubstantially, and that is God. He is eternal; He is.

This is what our Lord Himself replied to the Jews who said to Him: "Thou art not yet fifty years old. And has thou seen Abraham?" "Amen, amen, I say to you, before Abraham was made, I AM" (Jn. 8:58). By speaking thus of Himself, our Lord Jesus Christ affirmed His eternity.

But our Lord was indeed born in Bethlehem, hence He began. This is true. Yet, taken as a Person, our Lord, who is a divine Person, is eternal. He always existed. As man, by taking a body, He began in time. This is also a great mystery.

Did the Incarnation add something to our Lord, to the Word, and hence to God, since the Word is God? Certainly not. This seems incomprehensible to us, and yet it is true, because nothing can be added to God. That is evident. We find ourselves here in the presence of mysteries that are beyond us, but which are nonetheless realities.

These mysteries correspond to a necessity. There must be mysteries. It would, after all, be abnormal if there were no mysteries for us, because that would mean that we have nothing more to learn from God, and that our little knowledge would be equal to that of God, which is utterly impossible because the divine knowledge, like God Himself, is infinite, whereas ours is finite, limited.[24]

---

[23] *Ibid.*, p.22

CHAPTER 10

THE WORD IN THE BOSOM OF THE CHARITY OF THE FATHER

For us to become more attached to our Lord, to follow Him and to abandon ourselves to Him so that our lives become truly Christian, as He Himself so often demands in the Gospel, we need to try to understand better what He Himself is for us, as well as His work, His sublimity and grandeur. He must abide in us and we in Him.[25]

If we desire to appreciate what our Lord is, we must consider all the aspects under which He appears, and especially, first of all, in the Holy Trinity. How can the Gospel help us to better understand what our Lord is in the Blessed Trinity? One of the most significant passages occurs in the first epistle of St. John, when he speaks of charity (I Jn. 4: 12-15):

> No man hath seen God at any time. If we love one another, God abideth in us: and his charity is perfected in us. In this we know that we abide in him, and he in us: because he hath given us of his spirit. And we have seen and do testify that the Father hath sent his Son to be the Savior of the world. Whosoever shall confess that Jesus is the Son of God, God abideth in him, and he in God.

In a few lines, the apostle whom Jesus loved very clearly specifies the place of our Lord in the Holy Trinity and

---

24 But also because the intimate life of God, the life of the Trinity, as well as the Incarnation of God the Son, constitute an order of reality that is supernatural, as the First Vatican Council taught in its dogmatic constitution *Dei Filius*, on revelation. This supernatural order exceeds the capacity and the requirements of all created natures.

25 *Cf.* Jn. 6:57-58, and St. Paul: "For to me, to live is Christ, and to die is gain" (Phil. 1:21); also Gal. 2:20.

also in relation to us. By the simple confession of the divinity of our Lord, if it is made with genuine faith, God dwells in us, and we dwell in God.

> And we have known and have believed the charity which God hath to us, "*et nos credidimus caritati.*" God is charity: and he that abideth in charity abideth in God, and God in him (I Jn. 14:16).

Deus caritas est. It is good to meditate on this passage of St. John's epistle while asking St. Thomas what charity is.

St. Thomas defines the specific quality of charity in these terms: *bonum est diffusivum sui.*[26] Just as goodness tends to communicate itself, so too charity goes forth from itself, so to speak, from the person. Charity is generous. It would be contrary to charity if it were to hold something back, because it is the exact opposite of selfishness. Charity tends to give what it has and what it is. If then, this is what charity is, and God is charity, then in a way one can understand better why the Father engendered the Son, and that, from the Father and the Son, the Holy Ghost proceeds.

Since God is love, it is almost impossible for Him not to give Himself.[27] In giving Himself, He does it in such a way that, God the Father retaining nothing of Himself, the Son that He begets from all eternity is equal to Himself, the Father. No one can tax the Father with egotism or with having given Himself only partially. No, the Father has so given Himself in the Son that He has begotten from all eternity a Son equal to Himself without any difference or inequality. The only distinction is, exactly, that the Son proceeds from the Father; but the Father giving Him ev-

---

26 *Cf.* Denys, *De Divinis Nominibus*, ch. 4, §1, quoted by St. Thomas I, Q.5, A.4.

27 The processions of the Persons in the Holy Trinity are absolutely necessary, but without Revelation, we could not infer that God is love which burgeons into a Trinity of Persons.

erything from all eternity, the Son is exactly equal to the Father.

Clearly, it is a mystery. But the Scripture itself invites us to study what love is in God, since it defines God as being love, and the specific quality of this virtue is self-giving.

God is love, the Son is God, thus love is in Him, and it would be abnormal if nothing proceeded from Him, if He did not give Himself. The Father being love, if no other Person of the Trinity proceeded from the Son one might say that the Father is charitable, but the Son is not; that He is not really love, contrary to what the Gospel affirms.

Since God is love, the Son is also love. And from the Son there proceeds another Person, which represents the love between the Father and the Son: the Third Person, who is the Holy Ghost. This is the most perfect example of the love between the Father and the Son. And this Third Person, the Holy Ghost who proceeds from the other two is equal to the Father and the Son. In the interior of the Blessed Trinity there is the most perfect expression of love imaginable.[28] This trinitarian love is admirably expressed by the liturgy of the Feast of the Holy Trinity: "*Caritas Pater est, gratia Filius, communicatio Spiritus Sanctus, O beata Trinitas.*"[29] What commentary can surpass that of Dom Guéranger on this mystery:

> O delight of the Father in the Son, by whom He has the knowledge of Himself: delight of intimate love, of which He spoke to His creature man, on the banks of the Jordan, and on the top of Thabor![30]

---

[28] The Trinity of Divine Persons proceeding from one another, the Son from the Father and the Holy Ghost from the Father and the Son, corresponds well to the essence of love, but without divine revelation we could not know of the existence of these processions and of these divine Persons, ineffable culmination of the intimate life of God.

[29] Seventh antiphon of the Matins of the Feast of the Holy Trinity.

[30] *Cf.* Lk. 3:22; Mt. 17:5.

...O Son of God, Thou art the Word of the Father. Uncreated Word, Thou art as intimately in Him, as is His thought; and His thought is His Being. It is in Thee that this His Being expresses itself, in its whole infiniteness; it is in Thee that He knows Himself..."Thou art the brightness of the Father's glory; Thou art the figure of His substance" (Heb. 1:3). "Thou art the brightness of eternal light and the unspotted mirror of God's majesty, and the image that reflects His eternal goodness" (Wis. 7:26).

...Glory be to Thee, O Holy Spirit, who eternally emanatest from the Father and the Son in the unity of the divine substance! The eternal Act, whereby the Father knows Himself, produces the Son, who is the infinite image of the Father; the Father is full of love for this brightness which eternally proceeds from Himself; and the Son, contemplating the source whence He for ever comes, conceives for this source a love as great as that wherewith He Himself is loved. What language could describe this mutual ardor and aspiration, which is the attraction and tendency of one Person to Another in the eternally immovable Essence! Thou art this Love, O divine spirit, proceeding from the Father and the Son, as from one same principle; Thou art distinct from both, and yet art the bond that unites Them in the ineffable delights of the Godhead; Thou art living Love, personal Love, proceeding from the Father by the Son, the final term which completes the divine Nature, and eternally perfects the Trinity.[31]

[31] Dom Guéranger, *The Liturgical Year.* (Powers Lake, ND: Marian House, 1983). Vol. 10, pp.122-127.

CHAPTER 11

THE MISSION OF THE WORD SENT BY THE LOVE OF THE FATHER

These considerations based on the Gospel itself and on the simple notion of what charity is explain that the entire mission which has been given to our Lord and to the Holy Ghost is a mission of love. If God is love (*caritas*), what else can He do than give the charity that is within Him, not only *ad intra*, within Himself, but also in His operation *ad extra*, outside Himself, that is to say, in all creation, and with creation, in the Incarnation and the Redemption?

All that God has given to His creatures can only be the expression of His love. It is inconceivable that creation not be a work of love, and that creatures, especially spiritual creatures which God has created, not be in the reality of His love.[32] Thus, if we want to resemble the Blessed Trinity, to be closer to the Three Divine Persons, this can only be done in proportion to our own charity. We must become, so to speak, charity. Only if we could be defined, so to speak, as charity, would we really resemble God more.

This is easy to say, but it entails an entire program. That is why our essential and fundamental law is a law of love. This is the law that the good God has inscribed in our hearts, in our nature. This is the law of love which our Lord taught us. All the commandments are summed up in

---

32 "As God's favored children, you must be like him. Order your lives in charity, upon the model of that charity which Christ shewed to us, when he gave himself up on our behalf, a sacrifice breathing out fragrance as he offered it to God" (Eph. 5:1–2).

two commandments: Love God. Love your neighbor as yourself (*cf.* Mt. 22:40). In the measure that we accomplish this law of love which is in us, we are truly in the image of the Most Holy Trinity, God, who is love.

This is what our Lord Himself says in His priestly prayer, an admirable prayer worth rereading often. When He was alone with His apostles, our Lord expressed His love before manifesting it more concretely by His immolation on the cross. He showed it in the words which He first addressed to His Father:

> Father, the time has come; give glory now to thy Son, that thy Son may give the glory to thee. Thou hast put him in authority over all mankind, to bring eternal life to all those thou hast entrusted to him (Jn. 17:2).

And at the end of His "sacerdotal" prayer He says:

> Father, thou art just; the world has never acknowledged thee, but I have acknowledged thee, and these men have acknowledged that thou didst send me. I have revealed, and will reveal, thy name to them; so that the love thou hast bestowed upon me may dwell in them, and I, too, may dwell in them (Jn. 17:25-26).

Such is the love our Lord has for us: "...the love thou hast bestowed upon me," hence the eternal love that engenders the Son Himself, the love which is the very principle of the Son, if one can so express it.[33] "...[S]o that [this love] may dwell in them, and I, too, may dwell in them": the very goal of the love of our Lord for us is to transform us into love. It is in the measure that we keep His commandments of love, of charity, that we shall be in Him and He in us.

---

[33] The Son proceeds from the Father by way of knowing, as the Word of the Father; but in this eternal diction is involved the Holy Ghost, the mutual love of the Father and the Son, who prceeds from these two Persons by way of love.

What does this mean? Our Lord explains it when He promises to send His Holy Spirit, when He says: "I will not leave you friendless; I am coming to you" (Jn. 14:18). Our Lord identifies Himself, in some manner, to His Spirit which will come to us, the Spirit of love He will send us. And given the consubstantiality of the Father and the Son and the Holy Ghost, our Lord deliberately says: "The Father and I will come to you," and then, when He speaks of the Holy Ghost: "I will come to you when I send my Spirit." It is truly the indwelling of the Holy Trinity in us which effects this work of charity which is God Himself. He does nothing other than give us love.

Msgr. Gaume in his *Traité du Saint-Esprit* indicates, as far as it is possible to speak of this mystery of the Holy Trinity, our Lord's place and the mission that He is given:

> When speaking of the divine Persons, Catholic theology employs the word "mission" to signify the eternal destination of one Person of the Trinity for the accomplishment of a work in time. This destination is given to Him by the Person from which He proceeds. From all eternity, it was decided that the Word would become Man and would come into the world to save it: that is His mission. From all eternity it was decided that the Holy Ghost would come into the world to sanctify it; that is His mission. Thus among the divine Persons there are as many missions as there are processions. The Father does not have a mission because He does not proceed from any Person. The Son receives His mission from the Father alone because He proceeds from Him alone. The Holy Ghost receives His mission from the Father and the Son because He proceeds from them both.

These words are found in Holy Scripture. Worth citing too is the commentary about them made by St. Augustine:

> It is the Son who is sent by the Father, because it was He, and not the Father, who was made flesh. We also see that the Holy Ghost was sent by the Son, as our Lord said: "...if only I make my way there, I will send him to you" (Jn. 16:7); and by the Father: "...I will ask the Father, and he will give you another to befriend you" (Jn. 14:16). By this it is clear that nei-

> ther the Father without the Son nor the Son without the Father has sent the Holy Ghost, but He has received His mission from both of them. Of the Father only nowhere is it said that He was sent. (St. Augustine, *De Trinitate.*)

And the reason for this, once again, is that the Father is neither engendered nor does He proceed from anyone.

Moreover, in the Blessed Trinity, the fact of having a mission, of being sent, does not connote any inferiority in the One having received it relative to the One who gives it. St. Augustine writes:

> In Catholic dogma, the Father is not superior to the Son and the Son is not inferior to the Father.

The Son is sent by the One who has begotten Him, and the Father sends the One to whom He communicates being:

> Hence it is easy to understand that this attribute of being sent is given to the Son not only because the Word was made flesh, but so that he become flesh, and by his corporal presence accomplish the oracles of the Scripture. In this sense, the Son of God is not only sent as a man, the Word is sent in order to become man. (*De Trinitate.*)

There are two kinds of missions for the Son and the Holy Ghost, the one visible and the other invisible. For the Son, the visible mission was the Incarnation; and for the Holy Ghost, his apparition at the Baptism of our Lord, on Mount Tabor and on the day of Pentecost. For the Son, the invisible mission takes place each time He comes, Infinite Wisdom, Supernatural Light, to communicate Himself to the well-disposed soul, in which He dwells as in His temple. For the Holy Ghost, the invisible mission is renewed each time He comes, Infinite Love, Supernatural Charity, to communicate Himself to the well-prepared soul in which He dwells as in His sanctuary. The goal of this double mission is to assimilate the soul to the divine Person who is sent to him. O man, if only you knew the gift of God! In the divine thought, this mission is not transitory, but enduring. It is, in fact, as long as man does not put an end to it by mortal sin. It gives to the soul not only the light of the Son and the gifts of the Holy Ghost, but the Son and the Holy Ghost in person who come to dwell in it.

Chapter 12

The Procession and Mission of the Son

How the Holy Ghost effects the sanctification of the souls of the just is shown in an admirable book by Fr. Froget called *The Indwelling of the Holy Ghost in the Souls of the Just.*[34] The same doctrine is equally well explained by Fr. Bonsirven in *The Teachings of Jesus Christ.* He writes:

> Jesus never speaks directly about His Incarnation, but several times He states that He was sent by the Father, that He came from or went out from His Father. From these passages we can extract the following ideas: If the Son was sent by the Father, it is because before He was with Him and that He has, as it were, left in order to come into the world.[35]

Compare this to what St. John writes:

> If God were your Father, you would indeed love me. For from God I proceeded and came. For I came not of myself: but he sent me (Jn. 8:42).

The mission of our Lord is thus clearly expressed and it corresponds to His generation by the Father. The Son does not send Himself; it is the Father who sent Him. And yet, the general work of the Incarnation and of the Redemption, while attributed to or appropriated to the Son, is the common work of God. All three Persons participate in it. There has never been any work in which the Divine Persons were completely independent, even if there seems to be a certain appropriation of a work to one of the Divine

---

[34] Barthélemy Froget, O.P. (Paris: Lethielleux, 1900).

[35] Joseph Bonsirven, S.J., *Les enseignements de Jésus Christ* (Paris: Beauchesne, 1946) pp. 408–409.

Persons in a particular mission. St. John, in reporting the words of our Lord Jesus Christ, writes:

> ...you have loved me and have believed that I came out from God. I came forth from the Father and am come into the world: again I leave the world and I go to the Father (Jn. 16:27-28).

The passages just cited clearly show that if the Son was sent by the Father, it is because He was with Him and He has come forth from Him in order to come into the world.

It is St. John especially who enlightens us on the mission of the Word. He is the Evangelist who penetrated most deeply into the interior life of the Blessed Trinity. He was the recipient of extraordinary insights, as is seen from these particularly significant passages:

> And they have known...in very deed that I came out from thee: and they have believed that thou didst send me (Jn. 17:8).

> For this was I born, and for this came I into the world; that I should give testimony to the truth (Jn. 18:37).

> Jesus therefore said to them: Yet a little while I am with you: and then I go to him that sent me (Jn. 7:33).

> Do you say of him whom the Father hath sanctified and sent into the world: Thou blasphemest; because I said: I am the Son of God? (Jn. 10:36).

When the different passages of Scripture concerning the origin of our Lord are gathered together, it is striking to see the constancy with which He affirms that He comes from the Father, that He is sent by the Father and thus that He lives with the Father. These passages might tend to make us think that by the mission confided to our Lord, the Father separated Himself from the Son; that as He has sent Him, He has in some way become separated from Him. This is not so, and we must reject the thought, for, once again by the voice of St. John, our Lord Himself gives all the needed clarifications:

> And if I do judge, my judgment is true: because I am not alone, but I and the Father that sent me (Jn. 8:16).

> There are three passages from St. John, quoting our Lord, which show that He is not alone, but that He is always with His Father:

> And he that sent me is with me: and he hath not left me alone. For I do always the things that please him (Jn. 8:29).

The consubstantial union of the three Divine Persons is very clear, the fact that they are always together. They cannot separate. It is impossible to imagine that the Holy Ghost might separate from the Father and the Son, or the Son from the Father, for there is only one God; there are not three.

And St. John adds:

> Behold, the hour cometh, and it is now come, that you shall be scattered every man to his own and shall leave me alone. And yet I am not alone, because the Father is with me (Jn. 16:32).

These passages are suggestive. We must believe and profess that our happiness in heaven will be nothing other than the contemplation of the Holy Trinity, in the degree that we will be able to know Him by the light of glory that our Lord will give us. By the fruition in us of the sanctifying grace of our Lord, we shall participate, in a certain measure, in His glorious light which (in some manner) will cause us to enter the bosom of the most Holy Trinity to see and contemplate this infinite charity. Undoubtedly we shall not be able to understand, that is, be able to completely know the Divine nature. That is impossible. Not even the light of glory will be able to enable us to exhaust all the riches that there are in God, for then we should be God. But, as Scripture teaches us, we shall know God as He knows Himself. This does not mean that we will know Him in the same measure as He knows Himself, but in the same way, by the light of glory,[36] but, evidently, to a much lesser degree.

We know this also from St. Paul, who gives us as an example a star that differs from another by its light and brilliance: *Stella enim a stella differt in claritate.* For star differeth from star in glory (I Cor. 15:41). The same is true of the elect in heaven. They differ from one another in the abundance of this glorious light that they enjoy, and in the knowledge of God.[37]

[36] Participation in the Divine knowledge.

[37] Wherever there is a question of degree, of more or less, there is not plenitude, but only a greater or lesser participation in plenitude.

CHAPTER 13

THE MISSIONS OF DIVINE LOVE

Creation appears to us as an almost infinite universe, and yet its coming into existence changed nothing in God, added nothing to God, who is able to create worlds in infinite number. It is impossible for us to know exactly what God truly is, but how extraordinary it is that revelation has allowed us to know that there are three Persons in God. God is alone as God, but He is not alone as Person. There are three Persons in God.

God loves someone in so far as He can, to the degree that that person is lovable. God loves Himself much more, therefore, than He can love us, who are such limited creatures. By loving Himself, God begets a Person like Himself. It is truly extraordinary. These are the processions in God. We understand better why all creation is also like these processions, an effect of the love of God. The missions of our Lord and that of the Holy Ghost are also the effects of the love of God for us.

The first effect of divine love outside God, the first mission of love, was creation. By our Lord especially, by the Word, all was created, but also by the Holy Ghost (*cf.* Gen. 1:2; Judith 16:17). The result of this mission of love is that God created the world. And by the fact that we are created, we also have been sent, we too have received a mission.[38] This mission is neither more nor less than a part of the Word's mission, an infinitesimally smaller part, of course, as we are so little in comparison to the Word. But conscious of the fact that we have a soul, we have a known mission to fill, a mission of love. It is the same movement of charity that sends our Lord and that sends all creatures; material creatures without consciousness, and spiritual creatures with it. We are conscious of the love that abides in us by God, and by which we must walk.[39] Everyone has a mission on earth; if only everyone....

To think that God has created us, intelligent souls, endowed with will, conscious of the mission that we have to carry out on earth compels our admiration. Even if it is just a tiny mission, which seems insignificant to the eyes of men, it is a mission that has been willed from all eternity by God, in the Person of the Word and in union with our Lord Jesus Christ. This thought fills us with wonderment.

We can now attempt to define the mission of the Son. It supposes a prior state, or rather an eternal one, in which the Son and the Father are together in such a way that they are both distinct and consubstantially united: "In the beginning was the Word, and the Word was with God, and the Word was God" (Jn. 1:1). "I and the Father are one," says our Lord.

Then, one must take at full force the statement: "I came out from God" (Jn. 16:27). It means not only the eternal procession of the Son from the Father, but also the mission of the Son in time: "I came forth from the Father and am come into the world" (Jn. 16:28). In the first instance, the word "come out" shows the relationship of origin which constitutes the Person of the Son. In the second, it designates the Incarnation, which is the mission of

---

38 The mission is to sing the glory of the Creator, as did the three boys in the furnace (Dan. 3:51-90); or better, it is the mission to sing the glory of the Father of mercies "*in laudem gloriae gratiae suae*, to the praise of the glory of His grace" (Eph. 1:6). These human words of divine praise are but an infinitesimal echo of the divine Word who alone can adequately express the glory of the Father.

39 "And walk in love, as Christ also hath loved us and hath delivered himself for us, an oblation and a sacrifice to God for an odor of sweetness" (Eph. 5:2).

the Son. This is what St. Augustine explains, commenting on these words:

> He came out from God as God, as equal, as only Son, as the Word of the Father, and He came to us, because the Word became flesh in order to dwell amongst us. His coming is His humanity; His permanent state is His divinity. His divinity is the end towards which we are making our way, His humanity is the way that leads us there. That is why He has come to us without leaving God.

His mission is such that the Son is not separated from the Father, and He is able to say: "I and the Father are one" (Jn. 10:30). Jesus Christ and the Son who is sent are one and the same, as St. Augustine says: "He comes with the one from whom He comes forth."

We have read several affirmations that the Father is the author of the mission, and there are more. Jesus often uses the expression: "The Father sent me." This supposes that the Father is the principle of the Son; but given that the Son loses nothing of His oneness with the Father, with whom He enjoys complete equality, mission does not imply superiority. "No more so," says St. Cyril, "than a hearth would have to the heat and light that come from it."

The idea of mission, moreover, makes known the ministry of the Savior, Jesus Christ, which comes from the love of God. God is charity, and His mission comes from the love of God who wishes to save the world. Once again, it is St. John who admirably expresses this:

> For God so loved the world, as to give his only begotten Son: that whosoever believeth in him may not perish, but may have life everlasting. For God sent not his Son into the world, to judge the world: but that the world may be saved by him (Jn. 16:17-18).

If only men could understand this plan of love on their behalf. When one thinks how few there are among men who live this great mystery of the love of God and without knowing the mystery of the Holy Trinity and the mission of love of our Lord Jesus Christ, the reality of the Incarnation, of the Redemption, of the Cross by which we have been saved, one realizes the importance and the immensity of the task that belongs firstly to priests, to missionaries.

By the Cross we unite ourselves to our Lord in order to re-enter God, from whom we too have gone forth by creation. "*Creatio est a nihilo sui et subjecti*," theology teaches: creation is from nothing, both in itself and in the subject, which is to say that creation supposes the nothingness of the thing and the subject capable of receiving it. Thus, before creation, there was neither sea nor earth to support it: there was nothing but God alone.

God was, but we were not at all. Thus, we have been made out of nothing by God; which is not God's case, who was not created. He is always. He is. This sums up the radical difference between God and us. But by the fact that we have been created by God we emanate, so to speak, from His hands. We have come forth from the love of God.

We cannot be anything else than love. Those who lack charity are denatured.[40] It is against nature not to be love, so to speak. When we act selfishly, for our own satisfaction, to please ourselves, for our pride or self-love, it is against the end for which we have been created, and, even more, for which we have been redeemed.[41]

---

40 The absence of the supernatural virtue of charity comes from sin. Before the original sin, Adam and Eve enjoyed the love which accompanied the sanctifying grace which God had freely given them over and above their human nature.

41 Mortal sin robs us of charity and grace, and consequently renders our nature itself incapable of attaining its end, which is God, because this end is supernatural: it is the Triune God seen and possessed. This is impossible without grace.

We must constantly strive to focus on love, and orient ourselves according to the purpose for which God willed to create us. This is the basis of our spiritual life. For to the degree that we do not sufficiently love God or our neighbor, we are denatured.[42] This estrangement, clearly, is the result of sin, which has sown within us the spirit of disobedience, of defiance and alienation from God.

But having been redeemed and having received the Holy Ghost, the love of God, during Baptism when the priest said: "Depart from this soul, unclean spirit, and make way for the Holy Ghost," we must make way for the love of God which should reign in our souls. It is necessary to keep this love, and clearly this is the difficult part of the spiritual life. The consideration of love casts a real light on what we are, whence we have come and whither we are going.

The love which orders us to God must have as its object self-donation. This is done firstly by giving oneself to God. Even when we give ourselves, so to speak, to our neighbor, it is always for God and in God. Ultimately, there is but one love. There are not two loves, one of God and one of neighbor. The formal object of love is God, and that of the love of neighbor is identical: it is still God. There are two material objects of love, God and neighbor, but there is only one commandment, to love God. We love our neighbor to the degree that he comes from God or that he is going to God or is attached to God.

It is only in this perspective that we can and that we must love. We do not have a right to love our neighbor in so far as he separates himself from God by sin. We can only

---

[42] There is no middle ground between nature elevated to the state of grace, efficaciously loving God above all things, attaining the end for which it has been created, and nature without grace, turned away from God, thus incapable of attaining this end, and hence "denatured" in this sense.

love him because he is a creature who comes from God and who is destined to return to God, and because God is in him or so that God be in him[43] by grace. That is why we should love those who have received grace more than those who have not. We must love the others in order to give them God; because it is God whom we love in our neighbor. We do not love our neighbor for himself, but we love him for God. "Thou shalt love thy neighbor as thyself" (*cf.* Lk. 19:18; Mt. 19:19). Everything is taken up in this current of charity and love. This is the grandeur and beauty of our lives.

[43] *Cf.* St. Thomas Aquinas, *Summa Theologica*, II-II, Q.25, A.1 and A.1: "The reason for loving our neighbor is God, for what we must love in our neighbor is so that he might be in God...or for what there is of God in him."

CHAPTER 14

CHRIST THE KING

> I am come that they may have life and may have it more abundantly (Jn. 10:10).
>
> I am come, a light into the world, that whosever believeth in me may not remain in darkness....I came not to judge the world, but to save the world (Jn. 12:46-47).

From the consideration of the mission of Christ, we advance more deeply into the mystery of His Person. The coming of our Lord shows not only the goal of His mission, but it also presupposes the advent of one who was above and anterior to the world. It is really important to know our Lord, to know His mission, His origin, to understand whence He comes. Our respect for Him will be in proportion to our knowledge of Him. Undoubtedly, He assumed a human body and a human soul, but this does not diminish Him. Our Lord displayed sentiments of humility before His Father, but these sentiments do not diminish Him either, for humility is truth. When the Son says that He owes everything to the Father, He is simply recognizing the paternity of the Father to whom He is consubstantially united with the Holy Ghost from all eternity in the Holy Trinity.

To meditate upon the mystery of our Lord Jesus Christ and make it the object of our reflections may seem a little abstract or theoretical. And yet, upon closer examination, it is all together pertinent and practical. To define, so to speak, what our Lord is, to try to know Him better, to grasp better His relations with the Father in the bosom of the Blessed Trinity, the relationship of the Father and the Son, both His eternal[44] and temporal missions: all of this affects our own life, and I would add that it does so dramatically. For what is in jeopardy in the world in which we live is faith in the divinity of our Lord Jesus Christ. If our Lord is God, He is consequently the Master of all things, the elements, individuals, families and society. He is the Creator and the end of all things.

Once, before the beginning of a conference I was giving in Madrid, with about 5,000 persons attending, the crowd chanted incessantly, "Long live Christ the King!" We might ask why these people at that time felt the need to shout this in the street. It was because they felt that if Christ were not King in Spain, then that would spell the ruin of the Catholic religion and their own families. The Spaniards see every day, in the new laws and customs and habits of the people, that the Christian spirit is dwindling. They feel that our Lord is no longer King in Spain.

The same could become true for us. If we are not convinced of the divinity of our Lord Jesus Christ, we will not possess the strength to uphold our faith in opposition to the rising tide of false religions in which our Lord Jesus Christ is not King, is not acclaimed to be God. Nor will we be able to resist the consequences that this will have upon the morals of the State, of families and persons. But because of religious liberty, which was affirmed in the texts of the Second Vatican Council and which is entirely opposed to the social reign of our Lord Jesus Christ because it places all religions on a par and accords to error the same rights as truth has, our Lord is no longer considered to be the one Truth and source of Truth.

For instance, in Germany Joseph Cardinal Hoeffner, Archbishop of Cologne said "We are all pluralists here." Pluralists: What on earth does that mean? That means that

---

[44] Strictly speaking, that is His eternal procession from the Father.

our Lord is not supreme, that there is something besides Him. They grant that our Lord is someone, but also that He is not God. The way is then open to all opinions and to all religions. When such words fall from the lips of the Cardinal-Archbishop of Cologne, then the matter is very serious. It means that the Catholics who are accustomed to living in the midst of Protestants have definitively granted Protestantism the status of a "valid" religion.[45] They have lost the sense of the royalty of our Lord Jesus Christ, and by the very fact they implicitly lose the sense of His divinity. Hence it is a very serious lack of faith, and very little will be needed to cause people to draw away from the Church, give up the practice of their religion, and fall into an abysmal immorality.

At the beginning of the century the United States were held up as an example. It was alleged that the Catholic religion was making enormous gains because it is the land of liberty. Why wouldn't it be the same in every country? Let us grant freedom to all the religions—freedom of conscience, of the person, of morals. Then the Catholic religion, so the argument went, will have total freedom and will be able to expand. But this is to ignore the influence of error on truth, and immorality on morals.

It is true that genuine Catholicism made enormous progress in the United States, but, it must be recognized, a progress that was more spectacular than profound.[46] Big seminaries, Catholic universities, religious houses and Catholic schools were built. By the generosity of American Catholics there was an extraordinary flourishing of religious congregations. But look at what happened: The Church was shaken, it underwent a crisis, a grave one, and

---

[45] The plurality of religions in a state poses the danger of indifferentism; but this danger has never been so harmful as it has become since the ecumenism of the Council. Plurality becomes pluralism.

the whole structure collapsed because it did not have a solid foundation. There is no country where there were more departures from the priesthood and the religious life than the United States, where more radical transformations took place, for example, in the religious congregations.

This idea of liberty—which is really licentiousness and not true liberty—which is to be given to all the ideologies results in slow self-destruction and in the corruption of truth. And this truth is in fact our Lord Jesus Christ. Either one acknowledges it or not. If one refuses to acknowledge that our Lord Jesus Christ is the truth, by the very fact there is no more law and no more morality. Everything gives way little by little. Of course, it takes time. Christian civilization cannot be destroyed in the course of just a few years. But once the principle of liberty is granted, then slowly but surely the corruption advances. The number of divorces and divided families in the United States is unbelievable.[47] And ever since this liberalism has been intro-

---

[46] *Cf.* Leo XIII, Encyclical *Longinqua Oceani*, January 6, 1895:

> But, moreover (a fact which it gives pleasure to acknowledge), thanks are due to the equity of the laws which obtain in America and to the customs of the well-ordered Republic. For the Church amongst you, unopposed by the Constitution and government of your nation, fettered by no hostile legislation, protected against violence by the common laws and the impartiality of the tribunals, is free to live and act without hindrance. Yet, though all this is true, it would be very erroneous to draw the conclusion that in America is to be sought the type of the most desirable status of the Church, or that it would be universally lawful or expedient for State and Church to be, as in America, dissevered and divorced.

The fact that Catholicity with you is in good condition, nay, is even enjoying a prosperous growth, is by all means to be attributed to the fecundity with which God has endowed His Church, in virtue of which unless men or circumstances interfere, she spontaneously expands and propagates herself; but she would bring forth more abundant fruits if, in addition to liberty, she enjoyed the favor of the laws and the patronage of the public authority.

duced into our countries, the same thing has happened. The divorce rate increases at an incredible tempo, and then abortion, contraception and concubinage follow. Anything goes, it is total license.

The only remedy is to reflect, meditate, and be convinced of the necessity of the social reign of our Lord Jesus Christ, of His reign over us not only as persons, but also in society. Be assured that if you tell yourself that you want to live according to the law and the morality that our Lord has taught us, and by His grace, love and sacraments, but that out in the world you must accept freedom of morals and free-thinking, then sooner or later you will be contaminated. The mere fact of conceding that it is a human right to be able to think whatever you like, as is done in the declaration on religious liberty, leads to the abandonment of the missionary spirit. Make no mistake. It is completely erroneous to think that if someone thinks otherwise than I do, if he has another religion than mine, he is free to do so. No, he is not free, and we must tell him, however sorry we may be, that he is wrong, that he is not in possession of the truth. One day you will be judged on your thoughts, your behavior, and your attitude: you had better convert. And this holds, not only for ideas, but also for morals, for everything.

Our Lord Jesus Christ must reign, not only in our homes, but also outside and in all of society. Everyone belongs to Him. Everyone will be judged by Him. No man and no religion can hope to escape judgment by our Lord Jesus Christ. Our Lord Himself has said:

> For neither does the Father judge any man: but hath given all judgment to the Son (Jn. 5:22).

---

[47] In the US in 1996 there were 2,344,000 marriages and 1,150,000 divorces.

Because He is the Word of God, because He proceeds from the Father, He has a claim on all men. We must be convinced of the reality of these truths.

For the Protestants, liberty is first: everyone does and thinks what he likes. Having fought against the Catholics and having tried to suppress Catholicism, they know very well that Catholics hold that they possess the truth. Jesus Christ whom we possess in the Catholic Church is the truth. There is no other. This is what the Protestants cannot bear, knowing quite well that that is indeed what Catholics believe. Moreover, they cannot comprehend liberal Catholics who say: "You know, we all believe the same thing, we all believe in Jesus Christ; all that you think, we think too; you have the same sacraments as we do. Everything is alike. Let's make a common worship, and let the pastor come and preach to us and we shall go and preach to you." The Protestants do not agree. They know very well that it is not the true teaching of the Catholic Church, and that is why they hold us [traditionalists] in esteem. But they are afraid, for they know that we are intolerant. "You are intolerant," they accuse us.

Yes, we seem to be intolerant! Let's be clear: We tolerate error that cannot be suppressed, but truth cannot tolerate error. By its very nature, the truth casts out error as the light dispels darkness. We cannot help it. Truth does not tolerate error; good does not tolerate vice. This does not mean, in practice, that one does not tolerate what it is impossible to change, or what cannot be converted. But we should strive to bring an end to darkness, and to eliminate vice and error. And this is done by converting people by the grace of God. The whole missionary spirit of the Church consists in this.

To concede that everyone can have his own religion and that this is even a human right is extremely grave.

Firstly, it is not true. There is no right to be in error; there is no right, but rather tolerance. Of course, error is in the world, sin is in the world. Our Lord also said that there are weeds that grow with the good grain and that they will not be separated until the end of time. The former will be cast into the fire, and the others will be harvested into the barn, that is, into heaven.

We know that it is impossible to completely suppress sin; we cannot suppress ourselves. Of course, one tolerates sin as one tolerates oneself. But that does not mean that we put our virtues and vices on a par, saying that the ones are as good as the others. On the contrary, we fight against our vices, even though we know that we shall suffer from something until the end of our days. The point is clear: we tolerate ourselves and others. But we should pursue error and do everything to make it disappear. And society disposes of an immense influence in this domain, and we should undertake everything in order to christianize it or re-christianize it, because that is the will of God.

Institutions exercise an enormous influence on minds; when they are secular and atheistic they cause considerable harm. They cause the greatest scandal in the world, because it is organized error willed by the State, willed by society. So, with all the means they have at their disposal, they spread error. Error exerts so much power over minds that it is now impossible to find an important newspaper with a national readership that defends the Catholic Church and all its principles; which, in a word, integrally defends Catholic thought and faith.

There are practically none in Europe, because the entire press is in the hands of the big liberal anti-Catholic trusts, in the hands of Freemasonry. One saw in France, for example, the great change which took place from one day to the next during World War II, when Marshal Pétain came to power. He immediately suppressed Freemasonry: there was no more freedom of the press; pornography was outlawed and banished. All these things were banished immediately, and disappeared overnight. If France had remained like that, the society, without a doubt, would have been completely transformed. The serious sin, the capital sin, the mortal sin of General De Gaulle was to have let back into France Freemasonry, Communism, and everything that Marshal Pétain had banished.

CHAPTER 15

JESUS, THE WORD SENT BY THE FATHER

To express the mission that our Lord Jesus Christ came to accomplish on earth, the Gospel uses several terms. Our Lord says that He is sent by His Father (*cf.* Jn. 12:49). He also says that He has gone forth from His Father:

> For from God I proceeded and came (Jn. 8:42).

These terms: come, go, be sent, signify the same mission which, as St. Thomas Aquinas explains,[48] supposes an eternal procession in God. The Word can be sent by the Father because He proceeds from Him. His temporal mission is rooted in His eternal procession. In the affirmation of His mission and that of the Holy Ghost, our Lord affirms His divinity. This affirmation is based on the fact that He is engendered by His Father. To accept the mission of Jesus in the full sense of the word is to believe in the mystery of His Person, His divine Sonship, His Incarnation, His role of Savior.

We understand that by this affirmation our Lord expresses the central mystery of the Catholic faith. The words of our Lord found in the Gospel of St. John sum up, in a way, the faith: "For the Father himself loveth you, because you have loved me and have believed that I came out from God. I came forth from the Father and am come into the world..." (Jn. 16:27-28); ...and: "And they...have known in very deed that I came out from thee: and they have believed that thou didst send me" (Jn. 17:8).

---

[48] *Cf. Summa Theologica*, I, Q. 43, A. 4.

The Word proceeds from the Father eternally, and He has come into the world, He was sent.[49] The chief merit of the Apostles was to have believed this, and because of this belief they were assured of having their prayers answered and the Father's protection.

In the course of His words to the Apostles on the night of His Passion, the Son prays to the Father to grant His Church unity, sign of His divinity: "...that the world may believe that thou hast sent me" (Jn. 17:21).

Belief in the mission of our Lord means also belief in His divinity; and belief in His divinity, belief in the Holy Trinity, and this encompasses, in a certain way, the whole Catholic Faith. Thus by meditating on the mission of Christ, we gain a deeper understanding of the mystery of His Person. We grasp better how He presents His relations with His Father.[50]

It is necessary to point out a significant philological usage: the verbs expressing the relations of the Son to His Father are sometimes in the present tense, and sometimes in the past tense. Why? In general, it seems that the verbs in the present tense show the immanent relationship of Father and Son, that is, His eternal procession, whereas the verbs in the past tense either refer to the origin of this immanence, or else recall the Incarnation and its effects.

---

49 "From all eternity there is in God an essential communication by which the Father, in producing the Son, communicates his entire infinite and indivisible divinity to the Son. The Father and the Son together, in producing the Holy Spirit, communicate in like manner their own proper unique divinity to him. So also this sovereign sweetness was communicated so perfectly outside itself to a creature that the created nature and the godhead each retained its own properties while still being united together in such wise that they were only one self-same person" (St. Francis de Sales, *Treatise on the Love of God*, Bk.II, Ch.IV).

50 *Cf.* Joseph Bonsirven, S.J., *Les enseignements de Jésus Christ*, Beauchesne, Paris, 1946, p.412.

One might also say that, as time does not exist for God, our Lord can use either past or present to express the relations between Him and the Father in order to make Himself better understood by those to whom He is speaking, who live in time. It is very difficult for us to understand how this eternal present relates to creation in time and relations in time. As we read in St. John:

> And no man hath ascended into heaven, but he that descended from heaven, the Son of man who is in heaven (Jn. 3:13).

No one can speak of God if he has not seen Him, which supposes then an ascent into heaven. Only the Son of man knows God, because he came down from heaven and He is always in heaven, being one Person with the eternal Son, who never leaves the Father. That is why it is possible to say: "*Jesus Christus heri, hodie: ipse et in saecula*—Jesus Christ yesterday and today: and the same for ever" (Heb. 13:8), ...because He "sums up" all time by His Person, which is divine. St. John also says:

> Not that any man hath seen the Father: but he who is of God, he hath seen the Father.

The Jews understood quite well that the divinity of our Lord was being affirmed when He said:

> Before Abraham was made, I am (Jn. 8:58).

These are sentences that could not have been made up; only God could have uttered them. In his Gospel, St. John writes that the Jews took up stones to stone Him because He was claiming to be God. The Jews understood immediately what was meant by this use of the present tense. When Moses had asked God what he should say to the Jews if they asked him who had sent him, what his name was, God answered: "I am who am" (Ex. 3:14–15). God is He who is eternally. The Jews dared not even pronounce the word *Jahweh*; they wrote *Jehovah* and said aloud *Adonai*, because the name of God was too holy to pronounce. The name of this being who is and who remains forever seemed to them too sublime for them to even pronounce it. That is why, when our Lord said that He Himself was *Jahweh*, that He is who is, the Jews immediately prepared to stone Him to death. Most certainly, they understood what He meant to say.

The perfect unity of the Father and the Son is an abiding reality, belonging to the present moment. St. John expresses it thus: "*Ego et Pater unum sumus*—I and the Father are one" (Jn. 10:30). One is used in the neuter, expressing the unity, not of the Persons, but of the indivisible divine nature.

This is what our Lord says elsewhere, in one of these affirmations that it pleases Him to make, and which not even a very highly elevated soul enjoying divine favors would dare to employ: "The Father is in me and I in the Father" (Jn. 10:38). Only the Son, forever immanent in the Father, could utilize such language and say: "...I am not alone, because the Father is with me" (Jn. 16:32). All these considerations set us before a great mystery. The more we study our Lord and His attributes, the more we advance into an unfathomable mystery.

CHAPTER 16

WITHOUT LEAVING THE RIGHT HAND OF THE FATHER

How could our Lord have suffered the Passion? How can One who is God assume our flesh and truly suffer human pain while at the same time enjoying the beatific vision, which would establish Him in a state of ineffable happiness? How can He enjoy the beatific vision and simultaneously undergo martyrdom, feel such sorrow that it makes His sweat fall as drops of blood, and which compels Him to pray to His Father to remove the chalice, if it were possible? (*Cf.* Lk. 22:42-44). These are things both sublime and mysterious. Ultimately, it is the mystery of the love of our Lord Jesus Christ for us. For all that He underwent was for love of us. Of course, it is something absolutely unique....

In His Passion, our Lord's humanity is even more tangible, so to speak, than His divinity is during the Transfiguration on Mt. Tabor, for at the moment of the Transfiguration He was present bodily.

The Apostles who lived with Him had a greater sense of His humanity than of His divinity. They were slow to grasp His divinity, and that is perhaps true for us as well. While reading the Gospel or a life of Jesus Christ or even commentaries on the Gospels, we are more conscious of the humanity of our Lord Jesus Christ than of His divinity. It is necessary therefore to be prudent and to take care not to consider our Lord strictly by His humanity.

We must constantly make the effort to remember that our Lord is truly God, and that God is three Persons distinct but not separate. It would be an illusion and a serious error to believe that, the Father having remained in heaven and the Son having descended to earth, the Father and the Son were completely separated, or that, the Son having become incarnate, He would have been completely divided from the Father.[51]

The actions of our Lord are attributed to the Word, but it is the three divine Persons who accomplish them.[52] They are attributed to God; and there is but one God, there are not three. Here again we sound an extraordinary mystery.

Why then do we attribute to a single Person the actions which are accomplished by our Lord, when in reality they are the work of God, and not of the Word separated from God? The Word is never separated from God: the Word is God and consequently always consubstantial with the Father and the Holy Ghost. The solution is as follows: All the actions produced by His divine nature are accomplished by the Holy Trinity, even though they are attributed to the Word in a special manner; for example, the divine power effecting the Incarnation, or working miracles, *etc.* But the actions produced or endured by His human nature are attributed to the Word alone, and not to the Father or the Holy Ghost. Thus, it is the Word alone who becomes flesh, who suffers the Passion, who rises from the dead, *etc.* One must not fall into the opposite error, which would consist in having the impression that our Lord can be separated from the Father and the Holy Ghost.[53]

---

[51] "He came amongst us without leaving His Father; He was suckled by His mother, and He sustained the world. He was laid in a manger, and He was at the same time the food of angels. He was God and man at one and the same time: in Him He who is God is man, and He who is man is God" (St. Augustine, *Sermon 123*, no. 3).

[52] "But the Father who abideth in me, he doth the works. Believe you not that I am in the Father and the Father in me?" (Jn. 14:10-11).

Certainly, the apparitions which God made of Himself show us a kind of division, as, during the baptism of our Lord, the voice of the Father was heard and the Holy Ghost appeared under the form of a dove while our Incarnate Lord was physically present.[54] The voice is the Father, the dove, the Holy Ghost, and our Lord, the One who is Incarnate.[55] There is a tendency to consider the three Persons as divided, apart, separated from one another. Yet there can be no separation. There is distinction between the Father, the Son, and the Holy Ghost, but this is not the same as division.

All this is very beautiful, because we must think that all the actions accomplished by our Lord are indeed divine[56] and that they were done by the Word, by God Himself, and not just by someone who comes from God. No, it is God Himself who has come, and who has accomplished divine works. As I have already said, we have too great a tendency to see in our Lord just the man, because that is easier for us. St. Thomas says: "*Omnis cognitio venit a sensu*—All knowledge comes through sense perception." We are tempted to see in our Lord just His human nature. That is why it is good to emphasize His divine nature, as well as our Lord's divine Person, for in Him there is only one Per-

---

53 We sing in the hymn of Lauds for the Feast of Corpus Christi: *Verbum supernum prodiens, nec Patris linquens dexteram, ad opus suum exiens, venit ad vitae vesperam.*

54 *Cf.* Mt. 3:16-17.

55 With a difference, evidently: "Assuredly," says St. Augustine, "the creature in which the Holy Ghost manifested Himself was not assumed as were the flesh and the humanity of our Lord in the womb of the Blessed Virgin Mary" (*De Trinitate*, L, II, ch. 6, no. 11).

56 As the maxim of the *philosophia perennis* phrases it: *Actiones sunt suppositorum. Actions are performed by persons.* Hence all the actions of our Lord, those produced by His divine nature as well as those proceeding from His human nature, are divine because they have one divine Person as sole subject of attribution.

son, the Person of the Word Incarnate.[57] Since actions are attributed to the Person who accomplishes them, all that our Lord accomplished are divine.[58]

---

57 "...We say that the Word uniting with Himself according to person is a body animated by a rational soul, marvelously and incomprehensibly was made man....the divine nature and the human nature formed one Lord and Christ and Son for us, through a marvelous and mystical concurrence in unity" (Second Letter of St. Cyril of Alexandria to Nestorius, adopted by the Council of Ephesus in 431; *Denzinger,* 111a, *DS* 250).

58 Nestorius claimed to anathematize anyone "who tries to attribute [human] sentiments to the Word of God" (the human sentiments of Christ). To the contrary, St. Cyril of Alexandria anathematized those who "believe they must attribute (certain actions) to the man and certain to the Word alone" (St. Thomas, *Summa Theologica,* III, Q.16, A.4). In fact, what is said of Christ according to His human nature and what is said of Him according to the divine nature must both be attributed to the unique Person of the Word Incarnate.

CHAPTER 17

HE IS NOT FAR FROM EVERY ONE OF US

Our Lord, who is God, is the way that leads us to heaven. By the very fact that He is the Word Incarnate, He is omnipresent as God, as Word.[59] He is at the same time the Creator, and, consequently, He it is who maintains us in existence.

What is the difference between those who do not believe and those who do? between the demons and the baptized creatures that we are? The difference is not a matter of distance from our Lord Jesus Christ, of a certain physical separation: God is far from the demons, of course, because they reject Him; nevertheless, it is not purely and simply true. Our Lord Jesus Christ is not far from the demons because, being the Word, He is the Creator. And as such He created the demons and maintains them in existence.

This is what St. Paul says when addressing the pagan Greeks in the Areopagus: "*Quamvis non longe sit ab unoquoque nostrum*, Although he be not far from every one of us" (Acts 17:27). And he adds: "*In ipso enim vivimus, et movemur, et sumus*, For in him we live and move and are" (Acts 17:28). But there are two ways of being near. Our Lord may be near as Creator, but He can also be near by

---

[59] The sacred Humanity, however, is not omnipresent; the body of Christ is in its place in heaven, and also in the Blessed Sacrament. But in a certain way, His Humanity is present by His active power, in that it effects in us our sanctification as an instrument of His Divinity, either by hearing our prayers, or by interceding for us, or by shedding His graces. (*Cf. Summa Theologica*, I, Q.19, A.1).

love, by charity, by union with souls. In this sense, clearly, He is very far from the demons.[60]

Ultimately, if we try (as far as we are able) to think of what will be our spiritual life after death, the relations between God and ourselves, between all the spirits and ourselves, it is very difficult. And yet that is what is most important for us, what is most real. The spirit is much more real than the body, because matter comes from spirit. Consequently, it is the spirit which is infinitely more true and real.[61]

Thus, God is here present. Our Lord is in our midst. Not only does He hear us, but it is He who gives us voice with which to speak, eyes to see, and ears to hear. If our Lord were not present, if the Word, God, Creator, in whom all things subsist were not there, we would be nothing, we would dissolve immediately into nothingness. If our Lord is present, then, what difference is there between us and those who do not believe and the demons, since He is everywhere? The answer is that, in a certain way, our Lord's and our glances cross.

Remember from the life of our Lord in Palestine His meetings with sinners, the sick, and the apostles. Recall the words of our Lord to Nathanael: "When thou wast under the fig tree, I saw thee" (Jn. 1:48). But how? You have seen me? Was our Lord hidden?[62]

---

60 "The Lord is far from the wicked: and he will hear the prayers of the just" (Prov. 15:29). God said to Isaias: "...this people draw near me with their mouth, and with their lips glorify me, but their heart is far from me" (Is. 29:13; *cf.* Mt. 15:8).

61 "We are, then, in a world of spirits, and not just in the world of bodies which we see; and of these two worlds the most real is not the second but the first. And because only this one really counts, to tell the truth, St. Paul invites us to take just this one into consideration: 'Do not live on earth, but in heaven, *Nostra conversatio in caelis est*.' (Raoul Plus, S.J., *Dieu en nous*. Prayer Apostolate, Toulouse, 1937, pp.67-68).

Our Lord is there, with us. His eyes catch ours and question us. Do you really want to be with me? Do you love me? Do you not love me? Do you want to follow me? Or not? Are you with me, or are you against me? His glance says everything.

Remember the look our Lord gave St. Peter when he had just denied Him thrice. The Gospel says it: our Lord and St. Peter looked at each other, their eyes met. The gaze of our Lord fell on St. Peter (*cf.* Lk. 22:62). Think of all that is contained in our Lord's gaze.[63]

Our Lord is not far from us. He is with us; He is in us. Ultimately, everything depends upon the attitude we have towards our Lord. Of course, everything depends upon the grace of God, but everything depends upon our disposition to receive our Lord in us. Are we disposed to receive Him, or is there some part of us (a secret reserve) in which we would prefer that our Lord not enter, that His gaze not penetrate?

We are disposed to receive Him up to a certain point: in our mind. "May the Lord enlighten me, may He help my will."[64] But in my heart? Are there things which I love and which I know to be displeasing to our Lord? I would prefer that He not come; I would prefer that my heart not be illuminated by His gaze. I would risk seeing within myself things that I cannot keep. This does not sit well with our Lord.[65]

---

62 "Nathanael remembered having been under the fig tree, where Christ was not by his corporal presence, but by his divine knowledge." (St. Augustine, *De Verbis Domini*, Sermon 40).

63 "For Him, to look is to have compassion, because the mercy of God is necessary not only when one does penance, but also in order to do penance" (St. Bede the Venerable).

64 *Cf.* Ps. 17:29: "For thou lightest my lamp, O Lord: O my God, enlighten my darkness.

How different the dispositions of souls towards our Lord can be! Our Lord wants union with all of us, and to love us completely, without reticence. On His side there are no limits. His love is total, complete, perfect towards us. It is we who have a tendency to restriction. As St. Paul says: "*Dilatamini cor vestrum*, Be you [your hearts] also enlarged" (*cf.* II Cor. 6:13). Do not restrict them, do not narrow them or make them small in such a way that our Lord cannot enter in. Rather, expand your hearts, open them to the light of our Lord and to His love.[66]

Our Lord is always knocking at the door of our heart, as St. John says in the Apocalypse: "*Ecce sto ad ostium, et pulso*, Behold, I stand at the gate and knock" (Ap. 3:20). He knocks at the door of our hearts to be received, but is He received? This is not a matter of imagination or poetry; it is not literature; it is true.

And it is a fact. Consider what sort of people, in general, privileged souls have been, those who have received really extraordinary graces from our Lord, from God. They are the simplest souls; I would even say the most ignorant souls.

Our Lord Himself said as much of His apostles. He chose fishermen who were there in His path, who were simple men, not very cultivated. He chose them because in these men were simple souls, upright, who did not complicate matters overmuch, and who gradually opened themselves up to our Lord. Their hearts were completely opened to our Lord.[67]

---

65 On the contrary, the psalmist declares: "Who can understand sins? From my secret ones cleanse me, O Lord: and from those of others spare thy servant. If they shall have no dominion over me, then shall I be without spot" (Ps. 18:13-14).

66 *Cf.* Prov. 23:26: "My son, give me thy heart: and let thy eyes keep my ways."

Consider the saints in general. It can be said that our Lord really had a preference for poor simple souls, for children. Think of St. Joan of Arc, for example. Our Lord did not single out a highly qualified, highly intellectual person from high society with extraordinary natural talents. No, a simple soul.[68] And this is why, fortunately, souls which are not especially knowledgeable can be as holy as persons very well schooled in theology, in Sacred Scriptures, and in all of the sciences of the Church. It is moreover a great consolation to know that the love of our Lord for us depends upon the opening of our souls to receive it. That is all.

And it is on this point that we must always examine ourselves: "Have I not within me reserved areas which I do not want our Lord to see and enter, because if His light penetrates there I would be obliged to acknowledge the wounds that are still to be found in me, and which I do not want to heal."[69] Men are like that. How many Christians are only Christians by half? They say: "Yes, I believe in God, I believe in our Lord Jesus Christ," and thus they do their duty, what is strictly necessary to accomplish it. But ask them to make a retreat, to enter into silence and so be alone with our Lord, alone with the one who sustains them in existence, one on one with the one who gives them life, who gives them all and who will judge them. They flee. They are afraid that the secrets of their hearts

---

67 "Who shall ascend into the mountain of the Lord: or who shall stand in his holy place? The innocent in hands, and clean of heart....He shall receive a blessing from the Lord, and mercy from God His Savior" (Ps. 23:3-5).

68 In the humble of pure heart, the promise of our Lord is realized literally already on earth: "Blessed are the clean of heart, for they shall see God" (Mt. 5:8).

69 *Cf.* Jn. 3:19: "...and men loved darkness rather than the light. For their works were evil. For every one that doth evil hateth the light and cometh not to the light, that his works may not be reproved."

would be unveiled, whereas that would do them so much good.[70]

And that is why, during the course of the retreats, the confessions so often procure an extraordinary comfort to souls who really wish to make the retreat in sincerity and humility. "Once and for all I must give myself completely to God." Then God's light penetrates their hearts and His grace comes to their aid. They are free.[71] Such is our Lord.

We must reflect and consider that our sanctification is something really simple. It is not necessary to go and seek our Lord in metaphysical and theological meditations, or think that if you cannot understand theology very well you cannot sanctify yourself. Of course not. Normally, the more we study the mystery of our Lord, the more we should love Him, the more we should belong to Him. Unfortunately, often that is not what happens. Instead, we take self-satisfaction in our knowledge or in the natural gifts which the good God has given us, and we forget to humbly submit ourselves to the light of our Lord, to His love, to follow Him simply, to do His will.

It is necessary to recall frequently and meditate on this word of St. Paul: "*Non est longe*, He is not far from every one of us." "For in him we live and move and are" (Acts 17:27-28). May we be able to say: "My God, you are there; I love you. My God, I want only you. I want to live for you alone. You are my all." As St. Teresa of Avila expressed it: "God is all. I am nothing." That should be the cry of our heart and soul.[72]

---

70 "*Revela oculos meos, ne unquam obdormiam in morte,* Enlighten my eyes that I never sleep in death," the psalmist asks of God (Ps. 12:4).

71 They say with the psalmist: "Our soul hath been delivered as a sparrow out of the snare of the fowlers. The snare is broken: and we are delivered" (Ps. 123:7).

Let us live with our Lord constantly, in all of our difficulties, our trials, our desires; let everything be subject to our Lord. Let us never be found bereft and alone, when we might have the aid of Him who created us, who died for us on the Cross, and who comes into us (each time we receive Him) by His Body, Blood, Soul and Divinity.

---

[72] As the psalmist declares: "For what have I in heaven? And besides thee what do I desire upon earth? For thee my flesh and my heart hath fainted away. Thou art the God of my heart, and the God that is my portion for ever" (Ps. 72:25-26).

CHAPTER 18

FOR WHOM ALL THINGS WERE MADE

We have spoken about what can be called the "eternal mission" of the Word, as Son of God, inside the Blessed Trinity, that is to say, His procession from the Father. In addition, however, as Word of God, our Lord Jesus Christ is, in the order of creation, the one by whom all things were made. One can therefore say that God the Father also sent Him in the creation of all things. Of course, creation is the work of the entire Trinity. It is not the special work of the Word. The Father, the Son, and the Holy Ghost acted in the work of creation.[73] As the Son is the perfect image of the Father, He is also the model of all creatures. In Him were found, for all eternity, all the possibilities for creation, in its unity and diversity.[74]

---

[73] "We believe wholeheartedly and proclaim aloud that the Father, the Son, and the Holy Ghost, one sole God, of whom we speak, created, formed, governs and orders all things corporal and spiritual, visible and invisible" (Profession of Faith prescribed to the Waldensiens, AD 1208; *Dz* 421, *DS* 790, FC 241).

[74] *Cf.* Col. 1:16: "For in him were all things created in heaven and on earth..." About this St. Thomas Aquinas comments:
"The Platonists posited (eternal) ideas and said that all things exist only in so far as they participate in an idea....Instead of ideas, we have a single reality: the Son, the Word of God....In the same way that we say that the architect builds the house according to the plan that he has conceived within his mind, so do we say that God makes all things in His wisdom....This divine form and wisdom is the Word. It is thus that all things have been made in Him, as according to a pattern or model. '*Dixit et facta sunt*–He spoke and all things were made' (Ps. 32:9), because in His word, in His eternal Word, God made all things whatsoever" (*Commentary on the Epistles of St. Paul*).

Actually, the special mission of our Lord, the mission of the Word, in the mystery of the Incarnation and the Redemption, still goes on. It continues in the Church, in the priesthood, in the expansion of His mystical body and in the fight which this mystical body (given form in some manner by our Lord, by the Word of God) wages against the powers of hell, and against the might of the devil. Our Lord, however, is not, as Word, only the efficient cause and model of all things; He is also the final cause, for all things were made for Him.[75] It is St. Paul who tells us that everything was made for Him: not only by Him, but also for Him. Our Lord is the center and end of all things, of every creature.

In the Epistle to the Hebrews (2:10–11), St. Paul says:

> For it became him for whom are all things and by whom are all things....(this little sentence is very important),...who had brought many children into glory, to perfect the author of their salvation, by his passion. For both he that sanctifieth and they who are sanctified are all of one.

Thus, not only was the world created by the Word and by our Lord, but it was created for Him.

St. Francis de Sales speaks about this in his *Treatise on the Love of God*:

> Sacred providence determined to produce all other things, both natural and supernatural, for the sake of our Savior so that angels and men might serve him and thus share in his glory.[76]

The holy doctor emphasizes this point. He explains:

> Every well-ordered will that decides to favor several objects equally present before it loves better and above all the rest the one most worthy of love. It follows that when God's supreme providence formed his eternal purpose and design of all that he would produce, he first willed and loved with a pref-

---

[75] *Cf.* Heb. 2:10.

[76] St. Francis de Sales, *Treatise on the Love of God*, tr. by Rt. Rev. John K. Ryan, (Rockford, IL: TAN Books & Publishers, 1975) p.112.

> erence based on excellence the object most worthy of his love. This object is our Savior. Next, he willed and loved other creatures in order, according as they more or less pertain to his service, honor, and glory.
>
> Thus all things have been made for him who is both God and man, for which reason he is called "the first-born of every creature" (Col. 1:15): "possessed" by divine majesty "in the beginning of his ways, before he made anything" (Prov. 8:22)....[77]

St. Francis de Sales paraphrases the Epistle of St. Paul to the Colossians:

> For in him were all things created in heaven and on earth, visible and invisible, whether thrones, or dominations, or principalities, or powers. All things were created by him and in him. And he is before all: and by him all things consist. And he is the head of the body, the church: who is the beginning, the firstborn from the dead, that in all things he may hold the primacy.[78]

It is an extraordinary fact worthy of contemplation that all things were made for the incarnate Word. Everything that the good God made, all of creation—all creatures, archangels, angels, the history of the whole human race—all was made with our Lord Jesus Christ in mind. This is normal, after all, given that everything is for God, and everything returns to God by our Lord Jesus Christ.[79] As our Lord Jesus Christ, being God, has come amongst us, everything should be done for Him, and we ourselves are only worth something to the extent that we go towards Him, or belong to Him.[80]

---

77 *Ibid.*, p.114.

78 Col. 1:16-18.

79 "Christ...as man is our way to God" (St. Thomas Aquinas, *Summa Theologica*, I, Q.2, Introduction). "...[O]ur Savior the Lord Jesus Christ, in order to *save His people from their sins*, as the angel announced, showed unto us in His own Person the way of truth, whereby we may attain to the bliss of eternal life by rising again..." (*ibid.*, III, Prologue).

It is stupefying to consider the fact that most of the world lives separated from our Lord, and as if He did not exist. If only men had obeyed the order of our Lord Jesus Christ which He gave to the apostles: "Going therefore, teach ye all nations!" The apostles did all that they could because they shed their blood so that everyone could know our Lord Jesus Christ, and so that the whole world might be evangelized. But because of those who have betrayed our Lord, or who have denied Him, nowadays entire nations find themselves—and have for centuries—living without knowledge of our Lord.

And if all things have been made for Him, all things must be oriented towards Him and depend upon Him. By the very fact of the hypostatic union, our Lord has three essential attributes: He is Savior, Priest, and King. These three attributes belong to Him as man; they are proper to Him by nature, by His very constitution as God-Man. In our Lord there is only one person, the Person of the divine Word. By the very fact that the sacred humanity of our Lord—that is, His body and His soul—was assumed by this divine Person, the man, Jesus Christ, is Savior, Priest and King. This is normal; it flows logically from His existence, His being, and from the will of God.[81] Consequently, the world should be entirely subject to Him. Not a single creature or nation should fail to be subject to our Lord. This is how it should be, and we should be convinced that this is

---

80 That is to say, in the order of grace, where the members of His mystical body are united to their Head whether "by faith, by the charity of this life, or by the fruition of the life to come" (*Summa Theologica*, III, Q.8, A.3).

81 "The office proper to a priest is to be a mediator between God and the people. Now this is most fitting to Christ....He reconciled the human race to God, according to Col. 1:19-20: 'In Him (*i.e.,* Christ) it hath well pleased (the Father) that all fulness should dwell, and through Him to reconcile all things unto Himself.' Therefore it is most fitting that Christ should be a priest" (*ibid.*, III, Q.22, A.1).

so, so that we strive to bring about the reign of our Lord Jesus Christ, and for the continuation of His priesthood.

The final consideration is that our Lord is Savior. All peoples and nations should know that there is no salvation possible outside of our Lord Jesus Christ because there is only one Savior. We must be so convinced of this truth that we reject all forms of this false ecumenism that invents ways of salvation other than our Lord; which invents a priesthood outside of our Lord, and a kingship without Him, that is to say, the reign of man, the reign of the people—in a word, this false democracy which places the people in the place of God and of our Lord.

This is truly the modern heresy, which can be designated by a new term, for it really seems to be a new heresy in addition to modernism, liberalism, and all these old errors. It seems to me that this new heresy can be called ecumenism, false ecumenism. If there were to be a true ecumenism, it would have to be defined.[82] False ecumenism has it that the Catholic Church is not the only true religion. Men of the Church have invented a new ecumenical Church which places itself on the same level as other religions, which accepts all errors, and by that very fact secularizes all the states. The reign of our Lord Jesus Christ vanishes.

Thus, no longer can our Lord reign. He does not reign over the Moslems or the Buddhists. He does not even reign over the Protestants who no longer believe—or who scarcely believe—in His divinity,[83] and who certainly do

---

[82] Let us speak rather of true zeal for the union of Christians, according to the principle given by Pius XI in the encyclical letter *Mortalium Animos* (January 6, 1928): "The union of Christians cannot be procured otherwise than by fostering the return of dissidents to the one true Church of Christ, which formerly they had the misfortune to abandon."

not believe that the Catholic Church is the one true religion.

These considerations show why we must always return to the essential fundamental truths: What is our Lord? The great problem of humanity lies in the answer it gives to this question. Whereas for us who believe, it is extremely consoling, fortifying, and even invigorating to think that the one for whom all things were made is our Lord Jesus Christ.

---

[83] They do not admit the consequences which follow, whether for the individual–sanctifying grace–or for society–the social reign of our Lord Jesus Christ.

CHAPTER 19

A TWOFOLD MYSTERY OF UNITY

Before describing our Lord's psychology, and more particularly His human soul, and before discussing His relations with the holy angels and the elect in heaven, in so far as we are able and in as much as the good God has made it known to us, we shall try to penetrate more deeply into our Lord's interior life.

Our Lord's inner life—His spiritual life, his human interior life—matters more than His physical life. Without a doubt, the sacrifice of the Cross required that the Word assume a body capable of suffering and of shedding blood. But the oblation that our Lord made of His body could not have been accomplished without the interior acts of His understanding, will, and soul.[84]

One of the points dearest to the magisterium of the Church throughout the course of her history has been the defense of what our Lord Jesus Christ is. All the Christological errors, so numerous during the first centuries, were fought by the theologians and bishops who lived at the time. They defended the true nature of our Lord Jesus Christ, and especially the existence of His human soul, His human intelligence and will, against monothelitism,[85] monophysitism,[86] and against all the errors by which men have attempted to destroy our Lord Jesus Christ.[87]

---

[84] The visible sacrifice of His body supposed the invisible sacrifice of His soul, according to St. Augustine, who writes: "Every visible sacrifice is the sacrament, that is, the sacred sign of the invisible sacrifice. Now, an invisible sacrifice is the offering a man makes of his soul to God, according to this word of the Psalm (50:19): "A sacrifice to God is an afflicted spirit" (*The City of God*). *Cf. Summa Theologica*, III, Q.22, A.2.

The Church was at such pains to define the nature of our Lord that later (even though there have always been those who denied our Lord Jesus Christ, especially His divinity, as for instance, certain Protestants), one can say that within the Church and in her teaching, there were no more profound deviations on the subject of the nature of our Lord Jesus Christ.

One of the things our Lord most clearly affirmed was His oneness with the Father, and for us the contemplation of the oneness between the Father and the Son is a source of great consolation. To think that the eternal Son of the Father was present before the eyes of the apostles, criss-crossed the highways and byways of Palestine, dwelled in those lands, is a fact that absolutely consoles and encourages those who believe in our Lord Jesus Christ.[88]

It is a good idea to call to mind the words which our Lord spoke concerning His oneness with the Father, so that we might be perfectly convinced of this reality. We have already reviewed "the eternal mission" of our Lord, which is the procession of the incarnate Word within the

---

[85] The seventh-century heresy which denied the duality of wills and operations in Christ: distinct divine and human wills. Pope Honorius I favored this heresy and was anathematized posthumously by the Third Council of Constantinople (*Dz* 291; *DS* 552, 556; *FC* 359).

[86] The heresy of Eutyches, condemned by the Council of Chalcedon in 451 (*Dz* 148, *DS* 302). The monophysites asserted that the divinity and the manhood blend in Jesus Christ into a single new nature.

[87] Either by denying His divinity (Arianism), or His manhood (docetism, monothelitism, Apollinarianism), or the distinction of two natures (monophysitism), or their real union (adoptionism), or, finally, the personal unity of Jesus Christ.

[88] "He is laid in a manger, but he carries the world; He is nursed by His mother, yet He nourishes the angels; He is wrapped in swaddling clothes, but He clothes us with immortality; He is suckled by His mother, but at the same time receives the adoration of the world; He finds no room for Himself in the inn, but He prepares a temple to Himself in the hearts of the faithful; to communicate to weakness divine strength, strength reduced itself to this state of weakness" (St. Augustine, Sermon 190).

Trinity. This "mission" of the Word is eternal and continues, so to speak, is prolonged in time by the Incarnation.[89] This temporal mission instructs us about the eternal oneness between the Father and the Word.

In his work entitled *Les enseignements de Jésus-Christ*, the Rev. Fr. Bonsirven writes, as we have seen:

> From the mission of Christ, we penetrate more deeply into the mystery of His Person: "And no man hath ascended into heaven, but he that descended from heaven, the Son of man who is in heaven," says the Lord (Jn. 3:13).

This is a sentence that throws a vivid light upon what our Lord is. What is heaven? It is the Father who is heaven, it is God who is heaven. It is not a place where the Father resides. It is the Father Himself. It is God who is heaven. That is how it appears in the Apocalypse,[90] there will be no place.[91] God will be in all, and thus it is God who is heaven.

"...he that descended from heaven." Who then has descended from God? It is the Son of Man. He who stands

---

[89] St. Augustine sings a hymn of praise on the dual birth of Christ, His eternal procession and His temporal mission: "He is the revealer of His Father and the Creator of His mother, the Son of God born of the Father without a mother; the Son of man born of a mother without a father. He is the bright daylight of the angels, yet made Himself tiny in the daytime of men; the Word God before time, the Word made flesh in the fullness of time; the Creator of the sun, and Himself created beneath the sun. He governs the course of the centuries in the bosom of His Father, and consecrates the present day by coming forth this day from the womb of His mother; He always remains in the bosom of His Father, and He comes forth from the womb of His mother; Creator of heaven and of earth, He is born under the heaven on earth; ineffable Wisdom, yet wisely reduced to the silence of infancy. He fills the world and is laid in a manger; He governs the stars and is suckled at His mother's breast, He so great by His divine nature and so small in the nature of a slave, but without His littleness lessening His grandeur, and without His grandeur effacing His littleness. For by taking a human body He did not cease to accomplish His divine operations, nor to reach forcefully from one extremity to the other, and to dispose all things sweetly (Wisdom, 8:1)." (St. Augustine, Sermon 187, no. 3.)

before the apostles lives in the Father; He is in heaven. Our Lord can also say:

> Not that any man hath seen the Father: but he who is of God, he hath seen the Father (Jn. 6:46).

He who is of God, is His Son. St. John also writes this; it is once again the Son of God incarnate who can say: "I am from above," that is, from God (Jn. 8:23). Whereas His auditors are of this world, from "below."

He also says: "Before Abraham was made, I am" (Jn. 8:58),[92] signifying an eternal present. It was at this moment that the Jews took up stones to cast at Him. Manifestly, this was a clear assertion of His divinity. "The perfect oneness of Father and Son is also a current reality, belonging to the present..." says Fr. Bonsirven. And then comes this stupefying sentence: "I and the Father are ONE" (Jn. 10:30).

---

[90] St. John sees "a new heaven and a new earth" (Apoc. 21:1), then "the holy city, the new Jerusalem, coming down out of heaven from God, prepared as a bride adorned for her husband" (v. 2). Then he hears a strong voice from the throne, saying: "Behold the tabernacle of God with men: and he will dwell with them" (v. 3). In this city, St. John declares, "...I saw no temple therein. For the Lord God Almighty is the temple thereof, and the Lamb" (Apoc. 21:22).

[91] Save for the resurrected and glorified bodies.

[92] Jn. 10:30. St. Augustine comments on this sentence thus:
But that there may be no more room for hesitation, hear what follows: "I and my Father are one." Up to this point the Jews were able to bear Him; they heard, "I and my Father are one," and they bore it no longer; and hardened in their own way, they had recourse to stones. "Thy took up stones to stone Him." The Lord, because He suffered not what He was unwilling to suffer, and only suffered what He was pleased to suffer, still addresses them while desiring to stone Him. "The Jews took up stones to stone Him. Jesus answered them, Many good works have I showed you from my Father; for which of those works do ye stone me? And they answered, For a good work we stone thee not, but for blasphemy, and because that thou, being a man, makest thyself God. Such was their reply to His words, "I and my Father are one." You see here that the Jews understood what the Arians understand not. For they were angry on this account, that they felt it could not be said, "I and my Father are one," save where there was equality of the Father and the Son. (Commentary of St. Augustine, *On the Gospel of St. John*, Treatise 48, no. 8.)

Could He have affirmed His oneness with the Father any more clearly and perfectly?

These considerations should help us in our meditations and prayer when we are present before the Blessed Sacrament. We must have this clear awareness, this conviction, this profound faith that our Lord is truly God, that our Lord is in God, and is one with the Father and with the Holy Ghost. He is part of the Holy Trinity.

If we consider our Lord, we might say that (in a certain way) He is more God than man. Of course, our Lord is truly, fully man. He is a perfect man with a soul and body like ours.[93] He is even the most perfect of all men, but just the same, what gives subsistence to His manhood is God. It is the Word of God who assumes this manhood.[94] As God is so much greater, infinite, more perfect, more knowing than man, it is clear that the reality of God in our Lord is infinitely greater, infinitely more beautiful and deep, than His human reality. Yet nonetheless, by a mystery of the grace of the good God, a mystery of His love, we see the unity of this human creature—this human soul and body—and God Himself. They constitute but one sole Person in the two natures. Here too is a perfect oneness.

There have been heresiarchs who have taught that the two natures were separated, but made a unity of some

---

[93] The error of Apollinarius was to hold that in Jesus Christ the Divinity takes the place of a human soul. In the year 375 Pope St. Damasus condemned the proposition in these terms: "It is necessary to confess that (...) Wisdom Himself, the Word Son of God took a human body, a soul, sentiments, that is to say, the whole Adam, and, to be more explicit, all our old man, excepting sin" ("Letter to Paulinus, Bishop of Antioch," *Ds* 148).

[94] "Who, although He be God and Man, yet He is not two, but One Christ. One, not by conversion of the Godhead into Flesh, but by taking of the Manhood into God." (Symbol *Quicumque*, attributed to St. Athanasius, *Dz* 40, *DS* 76, *FC* 10).

kind.[95] The truth is that there is in our Lord Jesus Christ a profound and perfect, though mysterious, oneness between the human nature and the divine. This oneness consists in the one Person of our Lord, truly divine, the Person of the Word.[96]

It is clear that this reality had considerable influence on the human psychology of our Lord, and for the life of His soul. His human soul was united to God Himself, had been assumed by God. There was no other person. All the acts of this soul, as well as all the acts of the body of our Lord, were the acts of God. They were divine acts, because there were not two persons in our Lord, but one only.[97] The person is the subject to whom are attributed all our acts; consequently, all the acts accomplished by our Lord must be said to be divine acts.

---

[95] Fr. Gervase Dumeige explains it well: "The doctrine of Christ true God (*contra* the Jews) and true Man (*contra* the pagan gnostics) constitutes the foundation of Christology, which is established upon it by setting forth the truth of the hypostatic union: in Christ the divine nature and the human nature are united in a single divine Person. A substance or purely human personality in Christ would be incompatible with this unity (*contra* Nestorius). Therefore Christ does not add to his quality of Son of God a sonship of adoption by grace (*contra* adoptionism). (*La foi catholique*, l'Orante, Paris, 1982, p.179).

[96] The term *hypostatic union* signifies the union of two natures in one single hypostasis or one single person: the Person of the divine Word.

[97] All the human acts of our Lord are metaphysically the acts of God, from the fact of the hypostatic union. But psychologically, our Lord Jesus Christ was never conscious of anything without sanctifying grace and infused knowledge and knowledge of the beatific vision which illuminated His understanding. Full of grace and truth, our Lord had a full human awareness of His divine personality, and that His human acts were the acts of a divine Person. One sees how fitting it was that the grace of the hypostatic union be accompanied, in the soul of Christ, by the fullness of sanctifying grace.

Chapter 20

"I and the Father Are One"

Between our Lord and His Father there is perfect unity, as we have seen, and it could not be more perfect because our Lord is consubstantial with His Father. One of the most moving things is, perhaps, the way in which our Lord affirms His unity with His Father: "I and the Father are one" (Jn. 10:30). Of course this unity does not apply to the Person, because there are three Persons and that of the Son is indeed distinct from that of the Father; rather it applies to the community of the divine nature of our Lord and His Father; or more exactly, it applies to the consubstantiality of Son and Father.

Clearly, to correctly express the qualities attributed to our Lord is always delicate, and we must be careful not to make mistakes. When we speak of something which is attributed to or that is said of the Person (or the *suppositum* as the philosophers say, or the *hypostasis*, as the Greeks do), it is divine. It is attributable to God Himself.

The union in our Lord of the human and the divine natures, and the distinction between the Persons of the Blessed Trinity are great mysteries. All these things overlap: the activity of the Father, the activity of the Son, the being of the Father, the being of the Son and the Holy Ghost, the being of the Person of our Lord Jesus Christ and the activity of His Humanity....All this places us in a sphere that is difficult to define.

There are two great mysteries to consider here: the mystery of the Trinity and the mystery of the Incarnation as they are met with in our Lord; whence there results for us a difficulty of conception (and our imagination is always ready to trick us). However we may try to consider things in a purely intellectual, objective way, our imagination makes us see our Lord as if He were a human person. Undoubtedly He is a man, but He is not a human person. There is only one Person in our Lord, and this is the divine Person, and consequently everything that is said about Him is attributable to God and is divine.

So, when our Lord says to His Father, "And now glorify thou me, O Father, with thyself, with the glory which I had, before the world was, with thee" (Jn. 17:5), how can it be? The body of our Lord began in the womb of the Virgin Mary, it is true, but of Christ, with all the potential of His Person it can truly be said: "Jesus Christ, yesterday, and today, and the same for ever" (Heb. 13:8).[98]

St. Paul says of our Lord that He is eternal. When we speak of our Lord, it is of His divine Person united to His human nature; all the same it is our Lord who is eternal. It is difficult for us to express, but we must always come back to the fundamental truths of the being of our Lord Jesus Christ: His divine Person. The divine Person of our Lord is eternal: It was, it is, it will be.

The fact of being born in the womb of the Virgin Mary did not affect the Person,[99] just as the fact of creation did not bring about any change in God. Creation adds nothing to God, who would not have been perfect if it had added anything. In God there can be no change, no muta-

---

[98] St. Augustine expresses the permanence of the Word and the coming into being of the holy humanity He assumed in this manner: "The One who came forth as a bridegroom coming out of his bride chamber (Ps. 18:6), that is to say from the womb of a virgin, where the Word and the flesh celebrated a divine marriage, has worked a miracle in time, yet He is from all eternity; He is co-eternal with the Father, He is the Word who was in the beginning, the Word who was in God, the Word who was God (Jn. 1:1)" (*Sermon* 126, no.6).

tion, no increase or decrease.[100] God is perfect forever and from all eternity. He has His infinite being, and creation affects nothing in Him. Clearly, for us this is a great mystery; yet it must be so, or else we would fall into absurd conclusions that would lead us to say that God is not God.

Since the Person of our Lord is God, It has all the divine attributes: It is eternal, It is outside time and is not affected by the vicissitudes of temporal things. You see how great is the mystery of the Incarnation. It is very important to reflect on these things and to ponder them. We find ourselves enveloped by mystery, the great mystery, in fact, that our Lord revealed to us and which should fill us with joy and hope.

The eternal God truly united Himself to a human, physical nature in the womb of the most blessed Virgin Mary, but we must clearly understand that the human body and soul of our Lord would not exist without the divine Person. Everything in us only exists by means of and because supported by the person which the good God has given us and which is responsible for our being. Likewise, in our Lord it is the divine Person that has truly assumed this human nature in a perfect way. Whence it is true that our Lord can say that there is perfect unity between Himself and the Father, but it cannot be said that there is perfect unity and equality between our Lord's hu-

---

[99] The birth in time of the Word does not really affect the Person of the Word, but only according to our manner of conceiving things when we say "the Word became flesh." In reality, it only affects the nature that was assumed: "The human nature assumed is ennobled, but the Word of God Himself is not changed," teaches St. Thomas (*Summa Theologica*, III, Q.2, A.6), citing St. Augustine in his *Book of Eighty Three Questions*, Q.73).

[100] God is immutable: "I am the Lord and I change not," it is said in the prophecy of Malachias (3:6). That is because, being perfect, He can neither increase nor decrease in perfection (*cf. Summa Theologica*, I. Q.9, A.1). Moreover, "God alone is immutable, whereas the things which He made, because they are made out of nothing, are changeable" (St. Augustine, *De Natura Boni*, ch.1, cited by St. Thomas, *S. T.*, I. Q.9, A.2.)

man nature and God the Father. No, for then we would be excluding the Person, and we would be attributing to human nature divine attributes, which would be incorrect.

How extraordinary it is that our Lord can say to His apostles, in all truth and without deceiving them: "The Father is in me and I in the Father"; "I and the Father are one" (Jn. 10:38, 30). How extraordinary it is that a Person who appears outwardly a man can say such a thing! By the very fact, our Lord claims for Himself all the divine attributes: He affirms His eternity. He can say, "I have no beginning and shall have no end." It is true; our Lord can say this, because it regards the Person and not the human nature which does not exist by itself and which cannot be separated from the Person.

We have a constant tendency to divide our Lord and say that there is the Person of God and the person of the man. But this is an heretical viewpoint,[101] for there is only one Person in our Lord; we must always come back to this point. The Pharisees and the scribes said to Him, "You make yourself God, whereas you are only a man," and they wanted to stone Him. Their sentiments are understandable; they lacked the faith.[102]

It is good for us to meditate upon these little sentences that our Lord spoke to the apostles. They are of capital importance because they constitute the foundations of our entire religion. The Catholic religion is founded upon the Person of our Lord Jesus Christ. So that, if we begin to diminish the Person of Jesus Christ as the Arians did, for example, who said that our Lord was a very elevated per-

---

[101] Such is the heresy of Nestorius or that of the adoptionists.

[102] Unfortunately, pious Jews today think the same thing, as, for instance, the mother of Edith Stein, who said to her daughter as she was on the brink of entering the carmel of Cologne: "I don't have anything against Him...It is possible that he was a very good man. But why did he liken himself to God?" (*Edith Stein*, by a French nun. Paris: Seuil, 1953, p.134).

son, but beneath the Father, we would make of Him a created person and not an uncreated one. This is very dangerous, and that is why, by the very fact of this assertion, the Arians ceased to be Catholics; they had lost the faith.

Our Lord cannot be divided; He cannot be "dissolved." St. John incessantly repeats this point, especially in his letters:[103]

> Whosoever denieth the Son, the same hath not the Father. He that confesseth the Son hath the Father also (I Jn. 2:23).

He continues:

> Dearly beloved, believe not every spirit: but try the spirits if they be of God: because many false prophets are gone out into the world. By this is the spirit of God known. Every spirit which confesseth that Jesus Christ is come in the flesh is of God: And every spirit that dissolveth Jesus is not of God. And this is Antichrist, of whom you have heard that he cometh: and he is now already in the world (I Jn. 4:1-3).

All our faith and our strength consist in the affirmation of the divinity of our Lord Jesus Christ. The popes never cease to repeat it in their encyclical letters. That is why, in the encyclical *Humanum Genus*, Leo XIII condemned and excommunicated the Freemasons, as well as those who aid and abet them. The reason for this is their indifferentism towards all religions, which, in these sects, are all admitted

---

[103] Obviously, St. John, who lived in the first century, never knew the later heresies of Arius, Nestorius and others; but he did know the heresy of Cerinthus. According to St. Irenaeus, he taught that "Jesus was the son of Joseph and Mary, that Christ came into him at the moment of his baptism under the form of a dove, and that, at the end, Christ left Jesus to undergo the Passion and rise from the dead, whereas Christ, an eternal being, never ceased being impassible" (*cf. Adv. Haereses* I, 26). But if Jesus is not God, His Passion does not save us. Dissolving Christ, this heretic eliminates the Redemption. By denouncing Cerinthus, St. John becomes the precursor of all the holy bishops, councils and popes that, in the course of the following four centuries, will also condemn the heretics who "dissolve" Christ.

on a basis of equality. The popes, as well as all those who have the faith, cannot abide this.

We believe in the divinity of our Lord Jesus Christ, and it is this very reality that is directly called into question and attacked by indifferentism. We believe it is true that the Person of our Lord is equal to His Father, that He is truly the Son of the eternal God, possessing all the divine attributes—omnipotence, omnipresence, omniscience....our Lord is not a demi-god or a very perfect, supernatural man. No: He is God. If our Lord is God, then there can be only one religion possible here below and in heaven, that of our Lord Jesus Christ. There can be no others.

Those who have the faith (and who, like the popes, are responsible for defending it) are very sensitive to this definition, not because we must not love those who err, who have strayed into false religions, in order to convert them; but because it is quite another matter to give them the impression that our religion is equal to theirs, or that theirs is equal to ours. We can never assent to such a claim, because it would be a lie and a betrayal of our Lord. The Catholic religion was founded by our Lord Jesus Christ. Ultimately, it is His mystical body, the prolongation of our Lord who is God. There are no other gods. The reasoning is cogent, and no hesitation is permitted on this subject.

Nowadays we live in a climate of falsity, with a false ecumenism that undermines our holy religion, that diminishes it by trying to compromise. All the meetings with Jews, Protestants, Buddhists, and Mohammedans give the impression that we discuss on a par. But such a stand is not possible, and it does not depend on us. Of course, a certain equality exists because they are creatures like us; but as for us, we possess the truth.

The truth is that our Lord Jesus Christ is God, and everyone must be subject to Him. There is only one God to whom we must submit, our Lord Jesus Christ. We do not have the right to minimize this truth. We do not have the right, for example, to give a Moslem the impression that his religion is as good as ours. That would be a betrayal. Judas did nothing worse, and it was said of him: "It were better for him, if that man had not been born" (Mt. 26:24). If we too betray our Lord Jesus Christ, we run the risk of going to hell; we do not have the right to betray our Lord. This is something absolutely capital and fundamental.

The relations between the Son and the Father and the Holy Ghost (the Holy Trinity) are truly essential to our holy religion. They must be the object of our profound meditation and prayer: Adore the Holy Trinity, adore our Lord Jesus Christ, who is God.[104] Let us reread what St. John, reporting the words of our Lord in his Gospel, wrote:

> Do you say of him whom the Father hath sanctified and sent into the world: Thou blasphemest; because I said: I am the Son of God? If I do not the works of my Father, believe me not. But if I do, though you will not believe me, believe the works: that you may know and believe that the Father is in me and I in the Father (Jn. 10: 36-38).

---

[104] Once again, a sermon of St. Augustine will help us to adore: "How could He cease to be God by becoming man, who enabled His mother to remain ever a virgin, even during His birth? When the Word became flesh, He did not annihilate Himself by being transformed into flesh; rather it was the flesh, in order not to be destroyed, that was elevated to union with the Word. Man is body and soul; likewise Jesus Christ is God and man. It is the same One who, being man, is God; the same One who, being God, is man. There is no mingling of natures but unity of person. Let us repeat that the Son of God, coeternal with the Father who begot Him, wanted to have a beginning by being born of a virgin as the Son of man. Thus it is that the humanity came to be joined to the divinity of the Son, without, however, constituting a fourth person: the Trinity remains" (*Sermon* 186, no.1).

Once again, our Lord asserts His divinity in a very explicit way, and it is clear that no creature can validly make such a claim. He affirms His equality to the Father. And as I said, the Jews did not misunderstand; they understood Him quite well.

St. John also reports the reply that our Lord made to Philip when he asked Him: "Lord, show us the Father" (Jn. 14:8). "Do you not believe that I am in the Father and the Father in me?" (Jn. 14:10). And in verse 20, St. John adds these words of our Lord: "In that day you shall know that I am in my Father: and you in me, and I in you."

We must, then, have the profound conviction and and be able to communicate that what our Lord said—"I and the Father are one"—is the truth, which we must believe and love.

CHAPTER 21

WE HAVE SEEN HIS GLORY

The meditations that we have been making on the mystery of Jesus have allowed us to disengage ourselves from this world of contingencies, and lift up our minds to that world which lasts. As we have seen, our Lord clearly affirms His oneness with the Father, their consubstantiality, the integral community of nature and goods which the Son has received from the Father, unique Principle. He clearly affirms this, and nowhere more clearly than in His magnificent sacerdotal prayer, which we should read often. How rich it is, so consoling and so beautiful.

The first paragraph, undoubtedly the most beautiful, is like a glance at the Blessed Trinity itself:

> These things Jesus spoke: and lifting up his eyes to heaven, he said: Father, the hour is come. Glorify thy Son, that thy Son may glorify thee. As thou hast given him power over all flesh, that he may give eternal life to all whom thou hast given him (Jn. 17:1-2).

Our Lord thus asks His Father to give Him the glory which He Himself has given to His Father while He has been on earth, glory which He has also communicated to those whom the Father has given to Him. This refers to all those who have been His faithful disciples; and consequently, this applies to us, too.

Truly, these are words of eternity, admirable words which truly reveal who our Lord really is, the eternal Son of the Father. In this passage, the word "glory" is constantly on our Lord's lips. It is the word which captures or sums up what the Church believes and has always taught about eternity and heaven, about the Blessed Trinity. In the course of our prayers we constantly repeat *Gloria Patri et Filio et Spiritui Sancto–Glory be to the Father, and to the Son, and to the Holy Ghost.* We end the recitation of each psalm by "*Gloria Patri et Filio et Spiritui Sancto,*" making it more solemn and posed, because this prayer is the best thing that we have to say to the good God: Glory be to You!

What does this glory signify? Indeed, it is difficult to define, because it pertains to something eternal which is proper to God Himself, and because the divine Nature remains for us a great mystery. Still, I believe that we can say that this glory, this splendor—the honor which is due God—comes from the richness of the divine Being which contains all, which is the author of all, which is almighty, eternal, which is an infinite intelligence, an infinite spirit.

This spiritual radiance also has effects upon the body. Our Lord manifested it in His body during the Transfiguration (Mt. 17:1-9). But evidently it is especially a question of spiritual glory. Our Lord Himself says: "Now this is eternal life: That they may know thee, the only true God, and Jesus Christ, whom thou hast sent" (Jn. 17:3). Of course, we must not try to conjure up in our imaginations glorious rays of light such as the Apostles saw during the Transfiguration, but a spiritual radiance very much more profound, intimate, richer than this purely physical light. Our Lord asks that He receive back the glory that He had before the world existed.

But in fact, our Lord never lost that glory during His life on earth; simply, He did not allow it to shine forth in His body.[105] Possessing the beatific vision, and being the

[105] This glory is the attribute, not only of Christ's divinity, but also of His human soul as it is constantly beatified by the direct vision of God, the beatific vision. The normal consequence of the human soul thus glorified should be to irradiate the body, rendering it luminous, agile, subtle, impassible and immortal, like the glorified bodies of the elect in heaven (*cf.* St. Thomas Aquinas, *Summa Theologica*, III, Q.45, A.2).

Son of God, our Lord did not cease to be in the bosom of the Blessed Trinity, possessing the most perfect happiness in His whole soul, His mind, His understanding, His will and in His heart. It must not be thought for an instant that the Son failed to give glory to His Father, or that the Father failed to communicate His glory to the Son. But for the Apostles, our Lord did not appear on earth in glory.[106] He prays His Father to give Him this corporal glory by means of the Resurrection.

It is about this that St. Thomas Aquinas talks when he asks why it can be said of the Lord that He is seated at the right hand of the Father. He treats of the question under four points:

> ***(1)*** Whether Christ is seated at the right hand of the Father? ***(2)*** Whether this belongs to Him according to the Divine Nature? ***(3)*** Whether it belongs to Him according to His human nature? ***(4)*** Whether it is something that is proper to Christ? (*Summa Theologica*, III, Q.58, A.1-4).

For St. Thomas, and following the teaching of St. John Damascene, by the right hand is meant the glory of the Divinity:

> Hence, to sit on the right hand of the Father is nothing else than to share in the glory of the Godhead with the Father, and to possess beatitude and judiciary power, and that unchangeably and royally. But this belongs to the Son as God....(*ibid.*, A.2).

This sitting of Christ at the right hand of the Father can also be taken to mean the dignity communicated to the human nature of Jesus by the grace of personal union; or, better, as being

---

[106] If the glory of His divinity and that of His soul did not overflow into His body, this was the effect of a particular divine dispensation, St. Thomas explains, "so that He might fulfil the mysteries of our redemption in a passible body" (*S.T.*, III, Q.45, A.2); and also so that the Lord could "give men confidence in approaching Him by associating familiarly with them" (Q.40, A.1).

> ...according to habitual grace, which is more fully in Christ than in all other creatures, so much so that human nature in Christ is more blessed than all other creatures, and possesses over all other creatures royal and judiciary power (*ibid.*, A.3).

St. Thomas can then sum up and conclude:

> Christ is said to sit at the Father's right hand inasmuch as He is on equality with the Father in respect of His Divine Nature, while in respect of His humanity, He excels all creatures in the possession of divine gifts. But each of these belongs exclusively to Christ. Consequently, it belongs to no one else, angel or man, but to Christ alone, to sit at the right hand of the Father (*ibid.*, A.4).

And he adds one further consideration:

> Since Christ is our Head, then what was bestowed on Christ is bestowed on us through Him. And on this account, since He is already raised up, the Apostle says that God has, so to speak, "raised us up together" with Him, still we ourselves are not raised up yet, but are to be raised up, according to Rom. 8:11: "He who raised up Jesus from the dead, shall quicken also your mortal bodies": and after the same manner of speech the Apostle adds that "He has made us to sit together with Him, in the heavenly places"; namely, for the very reason that Christ our Head sits there (*ibid.*).

Think, then: if we cannot aspire to sit at the right hand of the Father because we are but poor creatures, nevertheless, through Christ who is the Head of the mystical body, we can have this privilege. Fr. Servien remarks:

> Whoever reads attentively the elevations contained in the sacerdotal prayer cannot but perceive the feeling of profound unity with the Father which the Lord possessed. The source of this perfect communion, which is expressed by the gift of the divine name and glory, is the love which is in God, which is poured forth firstly upon the only Son so as to extend by Him to other children of God. We are able to grasp the full import of the titles given to this Son: the beloved, the Only-begotten....[107]

[107] *Les enseignements de Jesus Christ*, pp.414-415.

While the term "consubstantial" seems too technical and philosophical to us, yet it is the only one that fits. It is because of His consubstantiality with the Father that all this glory is given Him, and that the Son truly shares in all the attributes of the Father.

On the subject of the glory of the Lord, Fr. Sauvé wrote in his work, *Jésus intime*:

> Heaven will be nothing other than the complete development and full flowering of the glory of Jesus. If we wish to take in this very important truth, which should give us a true notion of our Lord and also of our eternal union with Him, and of our eternal dependence upon Him, then we must consider it with faith and love according to its different aspects.

Fr. Sauvé then passes in review all the titles by which the Lord possesses this glory and communicates it to us, precisely because as man He is the Head of the Church Triumphant as well as, and even more perfectly than, Head of the Church on earth and in purgatory:

> As the divinity and the holy soul of our Lord developed His body during the course of His childhood and youth, with admirable perfection, by means of their eternal influence upon Him, so also His sacred Humanity, over the course of time, develops His mystical body, vivifying it and sanctifying it on earth, purifying it here below and in purgatory, while waiting for the coming of eternity, when It will animate the mystical body more perfectly and glorify it and beatify it for ever.
>
> Heaven will be nothing other than Jesus filling all the saints with His own life, His joy, and His glory: He will be all in all (*cf.* I Cor. 15:28).

These are beautiful passages which show how our Lord, in His glorious Humanity, communicates to us the glory He has received from His Father:

> O Jesus, how the role of Thy sacred Humanity fills me with joy; after having been my food here below, it will be, with Thy divinity, my life and my glory for eternity....How immense my folly would be were I to fail to draw now from this inexhaustible spring of grace and charity, every day and at

> each hour, and especially at the most fruitful moment of the sacraments, of Holy Communion, of absolution, so as to be able one day to possess more abundantly in heaven eternal glory and love. Jesus, the object of eternal delight of all the saints, Jesus, the model and source of glory, will be at the same time, by His Sacrifice, the soul of their adorations, praise and thanksgiving.

So much, then, are we able to say about the glory of our Lord, and the participation of it which we shall (let us hope) enjoy in heaven.

CHAPTER 22

THE HOLY GHOST, SPIRIT OF THE SON

After considering and meditating upon the relations of our Lord with His Father and the relations of the Father with the Son, and what was the glory of the Father and the communication of this glory to the Son, let us consider the relations of the Son with the Holy Ghost, the unity of the Son and the Holy Ghost.

This exercise is not without difficulty, and sometimes seems all too abstract during the course of mental prayer and meditation. To attempt to elevate our minds and hearts to the nigh inaccessible regions where the Blessed Trinity dwells and to place ourselves in Its presence, let alone to comprehend the bonds which unite the Lord, both Man and God, with His Father and the Holy Ghost, can seem to be too much to try. But for this we have the very words of our Lord in sacred Scripture, words which are very precise and which we cannot neglect.

The Holy Ghost plays a very important part in the accomplishment of the Incarnation. Of course, the Incarnation is the work of the entire Trinity, and not just that of the Word who became Flesh. It was to show this that the Father and the Holy Ghost were shown visibly united to the Son during the Lord's baptism.

It is especially in the Gospel according to St. Luke that most mention is made of the action of the Holy Ghost. We all have in mind the role of the Holy Ghost in the mystery of the Annunciation and the Incarnation. The Angel Gabriel replying to the blessed Virgin Mary explained:

> The Holy Ghost shall come upon thee and the power of the Most High shall overshadow thee. And therefore also the Holy which shall be born of thee shall be called the Son of God (Lk. 1:35).

This is the first mention of the Holy Ghost in the work of the Incarnation.[108] A little further on we read:

> And behold there was a man in Jerusalem named Simeon: and this man was just and devout, waiting for the consolation of Israel. And the Holy Ghost was in him. And he had received an answer from the Holy Ghost, that he should not see death before he had seen the Christ of the Lord. And he came by the Spirit into the temple (Lk. 2: 25-27).

From this it appears the it was especially the Holy Ghost who manifested the Incarnation; He effected it in the most blessed Virgin Mary, and He manifested its accomplishment through the old man Simeon. Once again, it is St. Luke who provides the account of the Lord's baptism:

> Now it came to pass, when all the people were baptized, that Jesus also being baptized and praying, heaven was opened. And the Holy Ghost descended in a bodily shape, as a dove, upon him. And a voice came from heaven: "Thou art my beloved Son. In thee I am well pleased" (Lk. 3:21-22).

And in the fourth chapter the evangelist adds: "And Jesus being full of the Holy Ghost, returned from the Jordan and was led by the Spirit into the desert" (Lk. 4:1). These few passages from the Gospel truly reveal what the good God has done for us. How can we not be filled with admiration when we consider how God desired to manifest the presence of the Holy Ghost, first, during the conception of Jesus, then again in the manifestation which was

---

[108] While the Incarnation is indeed the work of the three Divine Persons, it is appropriated to the person of the Holy Ghost by the Archangel Gabriel himself; and this, undoubtedly, because of the special resemblance of the grace of the Incarnation with the person of the Holy Ghost (*cf.* St. Thomas Aquinas, *Summa Theologica*, I, Q.39, A.8).

proclaimed by Simeon, and again during the baptism of the Lord, when He was manifested in a corporeal manner together with the words of the Father.

From this it is clear that it is not possible to affirm, as some do, that the divinity of our Lord Jesus Christ was not made clear in the Gospel until the very end of His life; or, even more so, that the Lord Himself was unaware of His own divinity until the very end of His life. Such an interpretation is utterly impossible, and yet this is what some of our modern theologians say.

These passages of the Gospel also give insight into the union that exists between Jesus and the Holy Ghost, as it is written, once again in the Gospel according to St. Luke: "And Jesus returned in the power of the Spirit, into Galilee" (Lk. 4:14). There is here a great immanence, so to speak, of the Holy Ghost in the Lord, an indwelling much greater than that effected by sanctifying grace.

The simultaneous presence of the three Persons in the blessed Trinity shows forth the equality of the Father, the Son, and the Holy Ghost; that is to say, the consubstantiality of the three Persons. Our Lord Himself affirms this in the Gospel according to St. John. Here the affirmations concerning the Holy Ghost are even more explicit:

> If you love me, keep my commandments. And I will ask the Father: and he shall give you another Paraclete, that he may abide with you for ever: The spirit of truth, whom the world cannot receive, because it seeth him not, nor knoweth him. But you shall know him; because he shall abide with you and shall be in you. I will not leave you orphans (Jn. 14:15-18).

In chapter 16, the Lord again returns to this subject:

> I have yet many things to say to you : but you cannot bear them now. But when he, the Spirit of truth, is come, he will teach you all truth. For he shall not speak of himself...(Jn. 16:12-13).

The sentences that follow express what is most characteristic of the Holy Ghost, and His relations within the bosom of the blessed Trinity:

> ...[B]ut what things soever he shall hear, he shall speak. And the things that are to come, he shall shew you. He shall glorify me: because he shall receive of mine and shall shew it to you (Jn. 16:13-14).

Previously, the Lord had spoken principally of His Father: "My Father will send him; my Father will communicate it." Here it is otherwise. The next sentences to follow in St. John's Gospel are truly mysterious and profound:

> All things whatsoever the Father hath are mine. Therefore I said that he shall receive of mine and shew it to you.

It is clear from this that the Son is equal to the Father: "All things that the Father hath are mine"; and so, to paraphrase, all that the Father gives the Holy Ghost to say is mine and comes from me, too. The Holy Ghost will receive what is mine. The intimate union of the Father, the Son, and the Holy Ghost is shown.

Truly, the reality of the blessed Trinity is the great mystery of the Faith. It is the affirmation of the divinity of our Lord Jesus Christ, and of the indissolubility of the Holy Trinity.[109]

We do not have the right to not confess the Father the Son and the Holy Ghost, or to separate one Person from the other (for example, to confess the Father only), because the Three Persons are consubstantial. St. John says it quite clearly in his epistles: Whoever divides the Son has

---

[109] There is no intention here to mingle the two distinct mysteries, that of the blessed Trinity, and that of the Incarnation; rather, their cohesiveness is being considered. It is on this point that some heretics err: Under pretext of not dividing the one Person of Christ, they divide the Trinity by diminishing the Person of the Son (as did Arius). Others, under pretext of not dividing the Trinity in the equality of Persons, divide Christ, by separating in Him God from Man (as did Nestorius).

neither the Son nor the Father.[110] In our Faith, it is not permitted to separate the Persons of the Blessed Trinity.

This has ramifications. For instance, it cannot be said, as we often hear said nowadays, that we have the same God as the Jews and the Moslems. People talk frequently about "the three great monotheist religions," placing them on the same level, as if we adored the same God! But by the very fact that the Jews reject Jesus Christ, by the very fact that the Moslems do not recognize the divinity of our Lord, neither the one nor the other adores the same God we do. It is absolutely impossible to say that they have the same God as we, because it is not true. From the moment you refuse our Lord, you refuse the Blessed Trinity, you refuse God. Our Lord Jesus Christ is not separated from the Father: They are consubstantial; there is only one God. From the moment you deny Jesus Christ, you no longer adore the true God.

It is unbelievable, but nonetheless a fact that these are commonplace errors, to be met with in the writings and in the words of priests, theologians, and even bishops! Even the highest authorities in the Church speak of "the three great monotheist religions"!

---

[110] *Cf.* I Jn. 2:22-23; 4:3.

CHAPTER 23

THE FATHER WHO IS IN ME DOES THESE WORKS

Not only is there oneness of Father, Son, and Holy Ghost, and communication amongst them, but it can also be said that the Father and the Holy Ghost acted in the Son, and that the action of the Father and the Holy Ghost was manifested in our Lord Jesus Christ. The Father is the Principle of all the operations of the Son. Here we must keep ourselves from minimizing the import of these words, as St. Cyril of Alexandria remarks. Fr. Bonsirven explains it thus:

> The operations that the Son receives from the Father are divine operations which a human nature could never do. Hence, it is not upon a man that they have been conferred, and it is not a man who claims a right to them: the Word merely assumes His eternal prerogatives; He does not receive what He has not. If He seems to petition something as if not possessing it, it is in order to show that the Father is the unique principle from which comes everything that the Son is. This special action of the Father on the operations of the Son is defined by two passages that it is necessary to unite: "...he that seeth me seeth the Father also. How sayest thou: Shew us the Father? Do you not believe that I am in the Father and the Father in me? The words that I speak to you, I speak not of myself. But the Father who abideth in me, he doth the works" (Jn. 14:9-10).

When Jesus justified Himself for working miracles on the Sabbath by laying claim to the Creator's power, He said: "My Father worketh until now; and I work" (Jn. 5:17). It is indeed a question of the same action.[111]

---

[111] That is to say, common to the Father and the Son.

> And when the Jews reproached Jesus for making Himself equal to God, He answered: "Amen, amen, I say unto you, the Son cannot do any thing of himself, but what he seeth the Father doing: for what things soever he doth, these the Son also doth in like manner. For the Father loveth the Son and sheweth him all things which himself doth: and greater works than these will he shew him, that you may wonder. For as the Father raiseth up the dead and giveth life: so the Son also giveth life to whom he will" (Jn. 5:19-21).

This communication of the life of the Father is complete, entirely at the Son's disposition, but the Son does nothing without the Father, because He receives everything from the Father. All the actions of our Lord, then, are truly divine. Commenting on these sentences of our Lord, Fr. Bonsirven explains:

> These sentences can only take on their full meaning when understood of the Son immanent in the Father. We find here two ideas. Firstly, God shows the Son all that He does: His divine operations, something which cannot be understood of the humanity of Christ. As St. Cyril explains, "show" does not mean to make someone see as in a drawing, but rather it means to be imprinted entirely upon the Son by the communication of the divine nature and operations; the Son exercises these divine operations because He possesses them by nature conjointly with the Father, but as receiving from the Father this activity. Moreover, the Son incarnate in time exercises them in succession: whence comes their manifestation in time, and the Lord's use of the future, which are consequences of the Incarnation.
>
> Secondly, by virtue of the immanence of the Father in the Son, by virtue of the Father as first principle, it is He who accomplishes in Jesus Christ His divine operations, not being content to give Him powers which he would exercise as if He were independent, as a separate cause.[112]

The Son, then, sees in the Father all His actions, and the Father accomplishes His actions in the Son, and yet it is also the Son who does them, consubstantially united to

---

[112] Rev. Bonsirven, *Les enseignements de Jesus Christ*, pp. 415-416 summarized.

the Father. It cannot be said otherwise, because they are not performed as an order that the Father gives to an inferior, and it is not a stimulus that is given to a secondary agent. It is in the oneness of the Father and the Son that the work is accomplished.

Understanding these mysteries is very difficult for us, because among created natures we find nothing similar to the oneness, to the consubstantiality of nature of Father and Son. Fr. Bonsirven concludes:

> All the actions of the Son: miracles, parables, judgment, vivification, are firstly the work of the Father. Who knows how to understand and look, will recognize this action as coming from the Father, because it is the product of the divine nature. He will discover, thus, God the Father present in the Son, not by a local presence, but as the archetype consubstantial with the Son and at work in Him.[113]

[113] *Cf.* St. Cyril, *In Jo.*, P.G. 74, c. 216 et 22, summarized by Fr. Bonsirven, *op. cit.*, pp. 416-417.

CHAPTER 24

THE PSYCHOLOGY OF CHRIST: CONTRASTS

We now begin to consider the subject of the psychology of our Lord. But let us be careful in approaching the extraordinary sanctuary which is our Lord's soul. When we use the term psychology, obviously it is with a special meaning. It denotes the study of our Lord's soul, His interior sentiments, dispositions, interior attitudes, His interior life. So doing, we enter a world which obliges us to meditate.

For it is not enough to meditate on our Lord in His divinity, as we have done, on His union with the Father and the Holy Ghost; we must find, in meditating on the soul of our Lord, a lesson and an example. For the reality is that our Lord is truly the model and the pattern of every man. It can be said without error that we have all been created[114] to the image of our Lord Jesus Christ, to the image of His holy soul and body.

When God decided in the eternal plan (before time was) to create mankind, what was its pattern? It was the humanity of our Lord, obviously. We are all created in relation to the Lord Jesus Christ, for Him, in order to be members of His mystical body. He is thus the model of our humanity.

Of course, when we turn our attention to the question of our Lord in His humanity, we are inclined to say that His case is extraordinary, unique. Consequently, we con-

---

[114] And recreated in grace, for those at least who have received the grace of baptism.

clude that He must be studied as an abnormal case. But so doing would be to create an illusion. Not only is His case not abnormal, but it is, on the contrary, the normal case *par excellence*, because He is the model of all creatures, the first born of all creation, the pattern of every creature.[115] Hence, we are not studying an abnormal case, but quite the contrary.

It is not because our Lord's soul was directly assumed by God, that it would not be a human soul. There has perhaps never been a soul as human as that of our Lord Jesus Christ, because by His divinity, by His omnipotence, by all the influence that God had on this extraordinary soul, He made it as human as possible, the most beautiful, the deepest, the most radiant, and so on endowed with every perfection of which the human soul is capable.

God gave to this soul possibilities which no other human soul will ever possess. There will never be another soul as privileged as the soul of our Lord in intelligence, in will, in heart, in all of His interior dispositions.[116] Yet nevertheless, this soul is indeed a human soul. That is why it is

---

[115] St. Francis de Sales explains this profound mystery: How God, having resolved to communicate Himself outside of Himself to a created nature in order to form with that creature one person, "the Sovereign Omnipotence...found it good to choose that humanity which later was actually united to the person of God the Son. For it He destined the incomparable dignity of personal union with His divine majesty, so that it might eternally and pre-eminently enjoy the treasures of His infinite glory" (*Treatise on the Love of God*, TAN Books & Publishers, Bk.2, ch.4, pg. 111).

Moreover, how, according to His sacred humanity, our Lord is the "first-born of all creatures," for in Him were all things created (*cf.* Col. 1:15-16), the same doctor also admirably sets forth: "The Supreme Providence then decreed that He would not restrict His bounty solely to the person of His beloved Son, but for that Son's sake He would diffuse it among many other creatures. Out of the sum of the countless number of beings He could produce, He chose to create men and angels to have company with His Son, to participate in His grace and glory, and to adore and praise Him forevermore" (*ibid.*).

good for us to meditate on the sanctuary which is the soul of our Lord, in order to try to discover what God, in creating it, gave us as our model and exemplar. To the degree that our own soul resembles our Lord's, it will be as God conceived it, and as God wants it to be.

Studying the psychology of our Lord, we meet with such contrasts, poles so far removed from each other that we wonder how there could be unity in the Person of our Lord Jesus Christ. In this soul were united seemingly irreconcilable elements: the uncreated and the created, the eternal and the mortal, the almightiness of God and the

---

[116] The Rev. Fr. Ceslas Spicq, O.P., speaks excellently of the soul of Jesus: "Sensitivity, delicacy of heart, strong emotions: these are qualities that every good son knows he has received from his mother. So it was from the Blessed Virgin that Jesus received the immense capacity for compassion that He displayed throughout His life. It was because He had such a lively sensibility that He could feel more acutely than any other man could, the trials which He underwent. Nonetheless He always kept His self-mastery...It is in such instances that one can comprehend what Christ owes to His mother: an inflexible will and sovereign liberty....His heroic will was the strongest that any man has every deployed. It was able to dominate, unflinching, the tortures of Calvary....[H]is soul ruled as undisputed master over His entire being, and from the moment of His birth He enjoyed absolute liberty. What He thought and wanted was never opposed by conceit or disordered passions, still less by external pressures. None was ever more "independent" of men and things....
It remains to give an idea of Christ's understanding....The more one studies the Gospels, the more one is stupefied by the appositeness, the quickness, the subtlety and the depth of the replies of Jesus to His adversaries. Jesus, having an extraordinary power of intuition and reasoning (*cf. Summa Theologica*, III, Q.12. A.1-2) could discover in the blink of an eye all the truth hidden beneath a phenomenon. His acquired knowledge developed with unheard-of ease and rapidity" (*ibid.* Q.9, A.4, ad.1).
And the same author explains that, born of a mother perfect and without stain of original sin, born virginally without a human father, Christ received a perfect body, and consequently a soul also perfect in its natural dispositions: "From the body of the Blessed Virgin a body very perfect according to nature was formed: for if the son is like the mother, then the more perfect the mother, so also the son." As the soul is the form of the body, the faculties of Christ's soul are also excellent, because excellently served by a physical nature most fine and perfect. (*Cf. Ce que Jésus doit à sa Mère* [*What Jesus Owes to His Mother*], Paris: Vrin, 1959.)

weakness of the creature, the infinite wisdom of God and the limited knowledge and wisdom of a human soul. We wonder at how, in one human being, the good God could unite such extraordinary things at one and the same time: perfect and continual joy and the most horrible suffering; sovereign peace and profound sadness. And yet that is what existed in the soul of our Lord.

In approaching the study of our Lord's soul, we may feel that it is a subject that it is not for us to study because we can never attain such perfection. We are sometimes inclined to think that it would be more profitable to meditate upon the soul of the Blessed Virgin Mary, of St. Joseph, of all the saints who are much closer to us since they are creatures like us, whereas the soul of our Lord completely surpasses us since it is irradiated by the Divinity. Of course, the soul of our Lord enjoyed the beatific vision from the moment of His conception. As soon as the Blessed Virgin pronounced her *Fiat*, the soul of our Lord Jesus Christ was created and was immediately placed in possession of the beatific vision.[117]

How then can we understand this Person who possessed the beatific vision and, at the same time, lived as we do?[118] Those who encountered our Lord in Palestine saw

---

[117] But such a most loving knowledge as the divine Redeemer from the first moment of His Incarnation bestowed upon us, surpasses any zealous power of the human mind; since through that beatific vision, which He began to enjoy when He had hardly been conceived in the womb of the Mother of God, He has the members of His mystical body always and constantly present to Him, and He embraces all with His redeeming love. (Pius XII, Encyclical *Mystici Corporis*, June 29, 1943, Denzinger, *The Sources of Catholic Dogma*, 2289; *cf.* St. Thomas Aquinas, Summa Theologica, III, Q.34, A.4.)

[118] "[Christ] was at once comprehensor, inasmuch as He had the beatitude proper to the soul, and at the same time wayfarer, inasmuch as He was tending to beatitude, as regards what was wanting to His beatitude, since His soul was passible, and His body both passible and mortal" (*ST,* III, Q.15, A.10). *Cf.* also *op. cit.*, *ST,* III, Q.34, A.3, ad.3.

Him as just another traveller, as any other companion for the journey, as any other dinner guest: the simplicity of the discussions and the conversations reported in the Gospels are the best proof of this. The human soul enjoyed the beatific vision, but in fact the Person was God Himself, with all the power and infinitude of God. These are extraordinary realities. Moreover, if we stop and think, this is exactly what God wants us to realize.

Our Lord took this soul and body in order to render glory to His Father, so that all creation might give glory to Him,[119] and in order to unite in Himself God, eternity, and all creatures spiritual and corporeal. All are united in the microcosm which is our Lord Jesus Christ. Thus all creation, by our Lord, rendered glory to His Father. But it is also for us that our Lord became flesh, that He came upon the earth and wanted to be our model. He thus wanted us to be like Him.

He wanted us, too, to participate in these things which seem almost impossible to assimilate. He wanted us to become gods. He Himself said it.[120] This is possible, of course, only to a small degree, but, nonetheless, it is so by a participation of the sanctifying grace that animated the soul of our Lord such that we, too, might have in advance the beatific vision through faith. The Faith is wholly di-

---

[119] The motive, or the proximate cause of the Incarnation was the Redemption of the human race: "*Propter nos homines et propter nostram salutem, descendit de caelis,*" we profess in the Creed. But the ultimate end of the Incarnation could only be the glory of God, by the recapitulation of all things in Christ: "Because in him it hath well pleased the Father that all fullness should dwell: and through him to reconcile all things unto himself, making peace through the blood of his cross, both as to the things that are on earth and the things that are in heaven" (Col. 1:19-20). "That he might make known unto us the mystery of his will, according to his good pleasure, which he hath purposed in him, in the dispensation of the fullness of times, to re-establish all things in Christ, that are in heaven and on earth, in him" (Eph. 1:10).

[120] Jn. 10:34.

rected towards the beatific vision. It is a stage, a temporary means which is already a kind of vision.[121]

The more holy souls possess faith, the nearer they are to this vision. The good Lord sometimes grants them a little ray of the beatific vision to elevate them even more. Such was the case of St. Paul, when he said that he had been elevated to the third heaven.[122] How, he did not know. Was it in his spirit? was it in his body? he knew not. What he knew is that he saw and heard things which human speech is incapable of expressing. He undoubtedly saw a little ray of the beatific vision which our Lord beheld in its plenitude.

This, then, is the goal to which we must try to direct our steps. It is for this that our Lord wanted to make us participate in His grace, and by that fact, in all His virtues. Meditation upon the soul of our Lord should give us the immense desire that He might more and more take possession of our own soul; that we might become, in some way, His other humanities.[123] This is what God wanted in creating us, that we should really be bodies and souls that our Lord, can, in some way, "invade," possess, direct, and in which He can sing the glory of God His Father, and fill them with His Holy Spirit. The good God created us so that our Lord might truly take possession of our souls; that it might be He who commands them, who takes them in

---

[121] Sanctifying grace is the beginning of eternal life (Jn. 1:14; Jn. 17:3), and thus a foretaste of the beatific vision.

[122] II Cor. 12:2-4.

[123] *Cf.* Blessed Elizabeth of the Trinity: Prayer to the Blessed Trinity (Nov. 21, 1904): "O my Christ, Whom I love....[I] beseech Thee to clothe me with Thyself, to identify my soul with all the movements of Thine Own. Immerse me in Thyself; possess me wholly; substitute Thyself for me, that my life may be but a radiance of Thine own....

"O Consuming Fire! Spirit of Love! descend within me and reproduce in me, as it were, an incarnation of the Word; that I may be to Him another humanity wherein He renews His Mystery!"

charge. This is what He does, this is what He wanted through baptism.

Once baptism has been administered to a soul, it is really the Holy Ghost, the Spirit of our Lord, who takes possession of it: "Withdraw, impure spirit, from this child, and give way to the Holy Ghost."[124] Contained in this there is a whole rule of life, a spiritual agenda that is certainly very enriching and at the same time very consoling to us.

The good God has really given us everything necessary for our minds to become other minds of Christ, for our souls to become other souls of Christ, for our bodies to become other bodies of Christ, so that the Word might, in a certain way, be incarnated again in us, so that He might guide us to our end: our end is the glory of God, which is the beatific vision, which is eternal happiness.

For this reason it is our custom to invoke the Blessed Virgin to help us to enter, however slightly we can, into the tabernacle which is the soul of our Lord. It is truly difficult for us to imagine what it could be, but the words of our Lord have been given to us. They make known to us the first reality that we discover in our Lord: His unity.

---

[124] Ritual of Baptism.

CHAPTER 25

THE PSYCHOLOGY OF CHRIST: HIS UNITY

Our Lord is truly one. We, however, because our faculty of understanding must dissect things first in order to make a synthesis afterwards, have a tendency to see in our Lord the divine Person and the divine acts on the one hand, and on the other the human nature and human acts. We seem to think of our Lord as acting sometimes as man, and sometimes as God; such a way of thinking is a great illusion.

Certainly, our Lord's actions are different, sometimes manifesting His divinity, sometimes manifesting His humanity.[125] His acts are "theandric," so to speak. It is necessary to respect the profound unity of our Lord, which is perfect. There are no divisions in Him. We must avoid thinking that in Him man and God are opposed in some way, for this is not the case at all.

The best proof of this is that our Lord, when speaking of Himself, says "I." The *I* which our Lord uses shows that in Him there is but one subject of attribution. All His acts,

---

[125] In our Lord there are two distinct principles of operation: the divine nature and the human nature; but there is a sole subject of operation, His divine Person. The acts that emanate from the divine nature are entirely divine, but the acts that proceed from His human nature are "divino-human" or "theandric." But in fact, the two natures are not compartmentalized, they communicate in their operations: "Dionysius places in Christ a theandric, *i.e.* a God-manlike or Divino-human, operation not by any confusion of the operations or powers of both natures, but inasmuch as His Divine operation employs the human, and His human operation shares in the power of the Divine" (*ST*, III, Q.19, A.1, ad 1).

all His thoughts, all the acts of love that He makes, all of His attitudes are all united in this *I* which signifies one divine Person, for there is only one Person in our Lord; everything is attributed to the divine Person of our Lord. The least human act, the least breath of our Lord is truly a divine breath, attributable to the Person. There is, then, no division in our Lord between God and man.

Fr. Bonsirven explains it thus:

> First, let's consider Jesus in Himself. The one we see speak and act looks like a man, outwardly like his brothers in all things; but he acts and speaks with the authority of a God. We cannot perceive any crack in his personality: it is perfectly one. Should we call Him God and man? The use of the connecting conjunction *and* threatens to break the unity. Let us say, following the received usage, a Man-God.
>
> The perfect unity is shown in that we find in Jesus a single *I*, a sole subsistence, to use the theologians' word, a single subject of attribution. This unique *I* is that of the eternal Son of God.
>
> Strictly speaking, we do not perceive in Him a human *I*, according to the dogmatic principle that teaches that the humanity of Jesus did not enjoy the normal completion which is the person; this role is assured by the Person of the Word. Nevertheless, the human nature of Christ exercises all the operations which are proper to it. We grasp better the exact relation between the two natures, the divine and the human. The common tendency is to place them on the same level, as two equal elements, as if they took turns as subject. But the Gospels give no indication of such an attribution or division.
>
> Moreover...speaking as the Son possessing nothing which He has not received from His Father, Jesus attributes His divine works to the Father who acts in Him,[126] who, in His everlasting love, never ceases to communicate to Jesus the divinity.

St. Thomas uses a very enlightening expression, which he says that he learned from St. John Damascene, to explain this relationship of the two natures: Christ's humanity is *instrumen-*

---

[126] "...the Father who abideth in me, he doth the works" (Jn. 14:10).

> *tum conjunctum divinitati,*[127] a perfectly docile instrument, because it is intimately united to the Divinity who uses it (*Les enseignements de Jésus*, pp.418-419.)

[The conference on this subject stops here. The reader may be interested in reading the conclusion that the editor believed it useful to insert, following the same pure line of Archbishop Lefebvre in the school of St. Cyril of Alexandria, St. Thomas, and Fr. Bonsirven.]

In our Lord there is a triple unity of operation: 1) First, the unity that attributes to the Father and the Son inseparably all the acts emanating from His divine nature, in the order of this divine nature, from the consubstantiality of the Persons; 2) Secondly, the unity that attributes to the unique person of Jesus, the Person of the Word, all the acts emanating either from His divine nature, or from His human nature, in the order of the subsistence, that is, in the order of the subject of attribution; 3) Finally, as a consequence of the second unity, a third unity that links to the divine nature of our Lord all the acts emanating from His human nature, not by mingling the two operations, human and divine, but by their necessary implication and intimate connection, according to what St. Thomas teaches following St. Cyril:

> Now it is clear that to be begotten belongs to human nature, and likewise to walk; yet both were in Christ supernaturally [since He was conceived by a Virgin and walked on water]. So, too, He wrought Divine things humanly, as when He healed the leper (Mt. 8:3) [an act of divine power] with a touch [a human action].[128]

---

127 "The flesh of Christ constitutes the instrument of the Divinity," says St. John Damascene (*De fide orthodoxa*, Ch. 15). But St. Thomas explains that he does not mean, like a separate tool, "like an ax or a sword," but rather like an instrument "assumed by and belonging to the hypostasis," as a man's body and members are to himself (*cf. ST,* III, Q.2, A.6, ad 4); or an "instrument united to the Word of God in the Person" (*ST,* III, Q.13, A.3).

128 *Summa Theologica*, III, Q. 19, A. 1, ad 1. The words in brackets are added to illustrate the text of the Angelic Doctor.

Fr. Bonsirven writes:

> This perfect unity and *synergy* of the two natures must exclude the questions one readily asks about the properties and activities of the Man-God: to which of the two natures do they belong? which would practically be equal to dissociating the two natures. There is not a single one of His operations,[129] not even the least physical gesture, that is not assumed by the divinity.[130]

He says "assumed by the divinity," not only by the divine Person, but also by the divine nature, according as the sacred manhood of our Lord is the choice instrument, the inseparable instrument, consubstantial, in the hand of the principal agent, the divine Word, according to His divine understanding and will.

---

[129] He is referring to the actions of the Man-God, as the Gospels report them, for example, and not the operations of the Word, such as the creation *ex nihilo*, out of nothing.

[130] *Op. cit.*, pp. 419-420.

Chapter 26

Humility Divine and Human

In the midst of our cares and worries, when trials and tribulations beset us, and especially in the painful times which the Church is traversing, our one great consolation is to be able to lean upon the only unshifting foundation: our Lord Jesus Christ. There is no other.

By studying the psychology of our Lord, and in particular the character of unity of His Person, we observed apparently dissimilar elements. It would have been easy enough to understand our Lord if He had only assumed a body and not a soul. Then one could have said that it was God who directly animated the body and who presented Himself to the inhabitants of Palestine and to the Apostles; that it was God in a human body.[131]

But such is not the case: our Lord had a human soul; in the mystery of Jesus we meet the presence of God in a human soul.[132] Did a division exist between this human soul and the Person of our Lord Jesus Christ? It is rather in ourselves that there can be a division since we are creatures animated by a human person, thus entirely distinct from God. In our Lord, this distinction did not exist because the Person who caused it to subsist was divine. There was in our Lord, therefore, a much deeper unity than there is between God and us.

---

[131] Such, in fact, was the heresy of Apollinarius (c.315–c.390), Bishop of Laodicea, condemned by Pope St. Damasus c.374 AD (DS 146).

[132] This thought finds expression in the Litanies of the Sacred Heart: "Heart of Jesus, holy temple of God, Heart of Jesus, tabernacle of the Most High."

We cannot separate ourselves from God either, since He is our Creator, since He it is who sustains us and who moves us at every instant of our existence, but it is not God who is responsible for our actions. Between God and our acts is the human person whom God Himself created and who is responsible for them. Whereas in our Lord, God Himself became responsible for all of our Lord's actions. The union between the soul of our Lord and God is infinitely greater than that between our person and God Himself.

Another aspect that is interesting to study in our Lord in order to better understand His interior life, is His humility. Among the Evangelists, it is St. John who studied the most our Lord's psychology, and who provides the words that shed light on the subject.

In St. John's Gospel there are passages that surprise us. If our Lord is God, how can He give the impression of humbling Himself before His Father? We would be inclined to think that this humility proceeds from His humanity, from the lively sentiment of being a mere creature. His body was created, His soul was also created: Is it in this sense that the Person of our Lord, by considering Himself in His human body and soul, humbled Himself before God the Father? Or can it be that the origin of this humility is to be found already in the life of the Blessed Trinity Itself.[133]

Certainly, the word *humility* can scarcely be applied to the life within the most Blessed Trinity. Nevertheless, if humility can be defined as nothing other than the truth, and if for us humility proceeds from the consciousness of having received all that we are and all that we have, in whom else can this consciousness be more vivid than in the Word who hears unceasingly: "*Ego hodie genui te*—Today I have begotten thee" (Ps. 109:3)?

This *today* is eternity. Our Lord is continuously begotten of the Father. Our Lord, the Son, feels Himself eternally indebted to His Father for His whole being, even though He too had no beginning and is equal to His Father. But the fact that He is the Son, hence begotten by His Father, causes in Him the recognition that everything comes to Him from His Father. This is true.

This is not a forced humility, it is not an imprecise sentiment, and our Lord expresses it very explicitly, not only because He has a human soul and a human body, but because His very divine nature comes to Him from His Father as well as His mission, and His divine knowledge.

It would be unthinkable that the Son who is God would not render homage to His Father by recognizing His Sonship. This piety is something very beautiful, and it extends to the humanity of our Lord. It is so much the more normal that our Lord humble Himself before the Father, as His human soul and body are evidently at a level infinitely inferior to the divine Person.

No one has spoken so well of the "humility of the Incarnate Son" that Fr. Lebreton in his *Les origines du dogme de la Trinité*:

> Upon opening the Gospel, one cannot help but be struck by the expressions of humility so new to Judaism and so strong

---

133 "It is said that He goes to the Father; this is according to His human nature. Hence when He says "He is greater than I," He does not say it as Son of God but as Son of man, by which He is not only less than the Father and the Holy Ghost, but even than the angels themselves (...). "But it can even be said, according to St. Hilary, that even by the divinity the Father is greater than the Son, without nevertheless the Son being less than He, but equal. For the Father is greater than the Son, not by omnipotence or eternity or grandeur, but by the authority of giving or of principle. In fact, the Father receives nothing from another, whereas the Son receives, so to speak, His nature from the Father by eternal generation. The Father is thus greater because He gives; but the Son is not less, but equal, because all that the Father has, He receives." (St. Thomas Aquinas, *Commentary on the Gospel According to St. John*, 14, 28).

> in all of those who approach Christ and who are led by His Spirit.
>
> But in contemplating Christ Himself, one perceives in Him, vis-à-vis His Father, a dependence, and even an annihilation, of which nothing here below can give an idea. His doctrine is not His own, nor His works, nor His life; the Father shows Him what He must say and do, and, His eyes on this most sovereign and well-loved rule, Jesus speaks, acts and dies. And this natural dependence of the Son of God is accompanied by an ineffable sweetness: as the Father gives all to the Son with ineffable love, so the Son places His happiness in receiving from and depending upon the Father.[134]

To me, this is a very beautiful sentiment, and which should make us reflect. If our Lord expressed this sentiment of homage and recognition of owing everything to His Father, how much more should we, who are so inferior to Him, also remain with the constant sentiment of owing everything that we are and have to God. And if each of us has a person which God wanted to create, who is responsible for our acts, that does not mean that we have less of a duty of rendering to God homage for what we are; on the contrary. We must, by our understanding and our will, submit ourselves to God, as our Lord did, but in a way even humbler, since our person is created; and in a way even humbler still, given our littleness and insignificance in relation to God and to our Lord.

If our Lord could not do otherwise than will what God willed, He still had two distinct wills. Monophysitism and monotheletism are heresies.[135] There are two wills in the Lord: one divine and one human. It is clear that between these two wills there could not be the least opposition. Such a thing is unimaginable, given that there is only one Person. Thus the human will of the Lord was always fully subject to the will of God.[136]

---

[134] [*Origins of the Dogma of the Trinity*] p. 312. *Cf.* Jn. 5: 19-20; 7:16; 14:10.

As our Lord did, and in the same way, we who have a human will must submit it to the divine will. Unfortunately, our will can, by a defect of our liberty, be separated from and even oppose God's will. That seems incredible, but that is, alas, the unfortunate reality.

By meditating upon this attitude of our Lord vis-à-vis His Father, we should try to find the model of our actions and activity:

> Herein lies what is most intimate in the Lord; and the more one penetrates the secret of this life, the better one understands the words of humble dependence which invite the disciples to rise to the source of life, of goodness, and of knowledge: God the Father. This trait, so clearly depicted in St. John's Gospel, far from compromising the divine filiation, can be seen as an essential element. He must not hide it from our eyes, but, on the contrary, reveal it.
>
> The pertinent passages in St. John's Gospel can be divided into two groups: those that establish the dependence of the Son, and those that show His unity with the Father. One

---

[135] Monophysitism, which teaches that there is one nature in Christ, was the heresy of Eutyches, priest of Constantinople, condemned by Pope St. Leo I (DS 290 ff.) and by the Council of Chalcedon in 451. Monotheletism, which teaches that there is but one will in Christ, was the heresy favored by Pope Honorius I....As Pope John IV later explained in his "Apologia for Honorius" (DS 496), Honorius actually meant that in our Lord there were not two wills in opposition. Still the explanation did not change the fact that to profess but one will in Christ was a heresy, which earned Honorius a *post mortem* anathema by the Third Council of Constantinople (DS 552) in 681.

[136] "*Ego quae placita sunt ei, facio semper*—I always do what pleases Him" (Jn. 8:29), our Lord says. During His Agony, Jesus gave full sway to the repugnance He experienced towards the Passion He was to undergo, all the while keeping perfect submission in His will: "Father, if thou wilt, remove this chalice from me; but yet, not my will, but thine be done" (Lk. 22:42).

The rational will of the Lord could not revolt against the divine will because it was impeccable, being the human will of the Word Incarnate; on the other hand, it was supremely free because full of grace, it always received a very strong and sweet actual grace, which, far from constraining its freedom, realized it, put it into practice as befits a free act (*Cf.* R. Garrigou-Lagrange, *Le Sauveur et son amour pour nous*. Paris, Ed. du Cèdre, 1952, pp.185-86).

might willingly conclude from them an incoherence (between the dependence of the Lord and the divinity which makes Him equal to God).

It is well worthwhile to make the effort to enter with the Evangelist into the deep current of Christianity in order to unite ourselves to Christ, to contemplate His life and enter into His thought: then one can feel the unity of the truth.

Later on, and especially after the fourth century, the theologians would show that the relations of origin and dependence are the only ones which serve to distinguish from one another the divine Persons, whose nature is common. Consequently, this dependence of the Son in relation to the Father, which at first glance seems to threaten the unity and even the equality of the two Persons, is, on the contrary, the thing that conserves it and enables us to conceive of it.[137]

A distinction is necessary, for if there were no distinction in God, there would be no Trinity. Because there are three Persons, there have to be relationships of filiation for the Son and procession for the Holy Ghost, and thus relations of total dependence. The Son depends on the Father for His whole being, but He never began. He has always been eternally. God is eternal and this engendering, to reiterate, takes place in an eternal *hodie*; hence, the Son is absolutely equal to the Father.

---

[137] Lebreton, *op. cit.*, pp.312*ff.*, 527*ff.*, quoted by Fr. Bonsirven, *op. cit.*, pp.421-22.

CHAPTER 27

OBEDIENCE DIVINE AND HUMAN

The study of our Lord's interior life can lead us into mysteries which at first glance appear contradictory; yet it would be impossible in fact for there to be contradictions in God's works, or, above all, in our Lord Himself. For instance, the fact of the coexistence of a divine and a human will in one and the same Person is a mystery: will this not entail a certain contradiction between the weakness, the limitation, of the human will, and the transcendence of the divine?...

This mystery should serve as a great model for us, as well as provide consolation. It is clear, as we have said, that there cannot be the least opposition between the two wills, for it is one and the same Person, the divine Person, who assumes the human will of our Lord's soul.

Speaking of our Lord, we always run the risk which I have pointed out, namely, of separating His humanity and His divinity, and then acting as if He were two persons. We must never forget that there is only one Person, the divine Person, who has assumed the human soul of our Lord. Nevertheless, the reality of His human soul remains, as do His human faculties, will and understanding.

Even in our Lord's words, there are things which seem hard to grasp. For instance, our Lord quite often affirms His own obedience. Can our Lord be said to be obedient? Indeed, He said so Himself[138] for one thing, and He became obedient unto death, even to the death of the cross.[139] Seeking the explanation of this obedience, we

---

[138] Jn. 14:31: "...and as the Father hath given me commandments, so do I."

might wonder if it is to be found uniquely in the fact that our Lord received a human soul. Or else we might seek the explanation in the fact that our Lord's human will is totally subject to the divine will, as it is the human will of the Lord's divine will, which proceeds from the Father. It is necessary, in any case, to keep in mind that the two wills are united; they can never be separated. Lastly, we might seek the explanation in the mission which the Father has given to His Son. He has been sent, and it is in accomplishing this order of the divine and temporal mission of our Lord Jesus Christ that this obedience occurs in our Lord.

Hence, the obedience of the Lord can be explained by the mission He received and which He accomplished, manifestly, under the influence of the divine will. He manifested this obedience when He said:

> Therefore doth the Father love me: because I lay down my life, that I may take it again. No man taketh it away from me: but I lay it down of myself. And I have power to lay it down: and I have power to take it up again. This commandment have I received of my Father.[140]

Our Lord says that He receives orders from His Father, yet it is surely not to be thought that within the Blessed Trinity orders are given by one Person to Another. Hence the only way in which the commands referred to by our Lord can be explained is by this mission. This mission is both eternal and temporal,[141] unfolding in time in the Incarnation of our Lord and in the Redemption. In time, the human will of the Lord takes up the relay, so to speak; all His human energy is drawn, as it were, from the mission

---

139 Phil. 2:8; see also Heb. 5:8.

140 Jn. 10:17-18.

141 It is eternal in the plan of divine Wisdom, in the communication of it by the Father to the Son from all eternity; but it is accomplished in time, "when the fullness of the time was come" (Gal. 4:4).

received by the Son from His Father, and obviously He carries it out faultlessly.[142] It is in this sense that He obeyed His Father, and in this sense that Christ's obedience must be understood. It is not inconsonant with His divine personality; it is an obedience both divine and human.

The Lord also says: "For I have not spoken of myself: but the Father who sent me, he gave me commandment what I should say and what I should speak" (Jn. 12:49). It is the Father, then, who prescribes what He is to say, by giving Him, in some way, an order which our Lord connects to His divine mission and to its temporal accomplishment. In this sense there is a prescription, and our Lord says that He always carries out the commandments of His Father (Jn. 8:29).

Even as He manifests His obedience, the Lord also shows Himself as possessing all power. Words of our Lord reveal this, as when He said to His disciples: "And you are they who have continued with me in my temptations: and I dispose to you, as my Father hath disposed to me, a kingdom" (Lk. 22:28-29). It is He, clearly, who prepares the kingdom. In this He manifests His omnipotence, He shows that by His will He can act, once again, not independently of His Father, but as His equal; He disposes of His Father's kingdom.

---

[142] It is especially in the Passion that Christ manifests His obedience animated by the love which He bears towards His Father: "But that the world may know that I love the Father: and as the Father hath given me commandments, so do I. Arise, let us go hence," namely, towards the scene of His Passion (Jn. 14:31). St. Thomas comments on this passage: "Christ suffered voluntarily out of obedience to the Father. From which it can be said (...) that the Father delivered up Christ to His Passion (...) inasmuch as, by the infusion of charity, He inspired Him with the will to suffer for us" (III, Q. 47, A. 3). Here it is a matter of Christ's human will. The source of our Lord's obedience is the fullness of grace in His soul, which itself flows from the mission of the Son of God, from the fact that, by His Incarnation, the divine Word pours out upon the holy soul of Christ the fullness of grace and charity.

This He also tells us in the magnificent priestly prayer which we have already cited, when He addresses the Father: "Father, I will that where I am, they also whom thou hast given me may be with me" (Jn. 17:24). It would almost appear that He imposes His will upon the Father; but we know that if He says this, it is precisely because it is also the will of the Father, and that their wills can never conflict: Perfect unity here exists, unity in the Trinity and unity in our Lord Himself.[143] We should strive to seek this unity. In order to be united to God, united to our Lord, our wills would have to resemble His and always be united to His. A beautiful example is here given to us.

Our will, of course, is not assumed by God, as the soul of Jesus is; nonetheless we too are sent, we too have a vocation; we must be faithful to the will of God. Our Lord is for us the model: Would that He might place in our wills the dispositions that He had in His own human will.

A passage from the Reverend Bonsirven develops the theme:

> If we consider the trinitarian life of the Father and the Son, we can understand their unity of will. The Father shows to the Son and communicates to Him all that He does. For His part, the Son neither wants nor can do anything but what the Father shows Him. What obedience can be as perfect as this integral communion, this uniformity of will? As St. Cyril explains in a rather lovely image, we can no more say that there are real commands given from Father to Son, than we could say that the sun commands its rays to shine. And the same Doctor adds that if we consider the Word Incarnate, the commandment referred to is not the order of a superior, but uniquely the expression of the Son's mission.

Let us say more exactly that from the Father to the Son there is no real commandment, but mission of the Person

---

143 The Father and the Son have only one and the same will. As for Christ, His human will is always in conformity to His divine will, which is also that of His Father.

of the Son; and if we are considering the Son Incarnate, the commandment and the obedience express at the same time the eternal mission and its accomplishment in time, in particular by His human will and operation. The Reverend Bonsirven explains:

> This attitude of free dependence appears in a well-known scene. The two sons of Zebedee approach Jesus and ask Him to grant them to sit in the two highest places in the kingdom, on His right hand and on His left. Jesus answers: "You know not what you ask. Can you drink the chalice that I shall drink? They say to him: We can." Jesus replies: "My chalice indeed you shall drink; but to sit on my right or left hand is not mine to give to you, but to them for whom it is prepared by my Father."[144]
>
> By this answer, Christ did not seek to elude an importunate request, still less did he wish to deny what He affirms elsewhere, that He has the right to dispose of the kingdom and that in fact He does dispose of it in favor of His own; but He wanted to remind His presumptuous apostles that all these graces come from the Father as from the first source, and that it is from Him that they should humbly seek them.[145]

Even here there is no contradiction between our Lord's affirmations, but He wanted to remind the sons of Zebedee of humility, and that everything comes first of all from the Father, and that He Himself receives everything from the Father and submits Himself to His Father.

---

[144] Mt. 20:22-23.
[145] Bonsirven, *Les enseignements de Jésus*, p. 424.

CHAPTER 28

THE MAN OF SORROWS

If the reality of two wills in our Lord as presented in passages of the Gospels poses a difficulty to our minds, there is a reality more mysterious still: the fact that our Lord could suffer in His will and in His human soul, even though consubstantially united to God. The depth of the mystery is expressed by Fr. Bonsirven:

> His unshakable, unchangeable resolution of loving obedience, while guaranteeing substantial holiness and a strict moral union of His wills, did not suppress the experience of interior sufferings and trials.[146]

The Passion of the Savior is a great mystery.

All the spiritual writers and all the theologians concur in saying that no one could suffer as much as our Lord Jesus Christ suffered; yet the great mystery is that He could suffer while at the same time being rendered happy by the possession of the beatific vision in His human soul. St. Thomas Aquinas addresses this matter in questions 46–49 of the third part of the *Summa*, and also in his *Compendium Theologiae*:

> If there were sadness in Christ, then the other passions that are born of sadness were present also, as fear, anger, *etc.* The presence of that by which sadness is engendered in our soul also causes fear when we see an evil to come; and we become angry against someone whose blows have saddened us. Nevertheless, these passions in Christ were in a different way than they are in us. In us, most of the time, these passions precede

---

[146] The Rev. Bonsirven, *Les enseignements de Jesus*, p. 425. Moreover, as Fr. Garrigou-Lagrange taught, "Fullness of grace caused within our Lord an ardent desire of the cross for the perfect accomplishment of His mission of redemption" (*The Love of God and the Cross of Jesus*, p. 208 sq.)

> the judgment of reason (...), whereas in Christ they never exceeded the mode and manner fixed by reason; rather the inferior appetite, which is subject to passion, was not moved save in the measure ordained by reason. It could happen that the soul of Christ, in His inferior reason, refused what, in the superior reason, He desired.[147]

St. Thomas makes a distinction between the inferior reason which governs the senses and the body, and the superior reason which reaches God and lives with God and in God.

> There was not in Him, however, any annoyance of appetites or rebellion of the flesh against the spirit. This rebellion occurs in us because the inferior appetite outstrips the judgment or transgresses the rule of reason; but in Christ, the inferior appetite was governed by the judgment of reason, for He allowed each of His lower faculties to follow its own movement only in the measure that He willed. In light of these considerations, it is clear that the superior reason of Christ fully experienced the pleasure and the enjoyment of its object: the beatific vision. For this reason nothing could happen to Him which would be a cause of sadness. The enjoyment of the beatific vision did not diminish Christ's Passion, nor did the Passion prevent this enjoyment, since there was no influence felt of one faculty upon the other, and each faculty was restricted to its proper object.

It is in His inferior faculty, then, that our Lord suffered, and this explains the words which He spoke: "Let this chalice pass me by." Fr. Synave comments on this:

> To this explanation of St. Thomas on the coexistence in the soul of Christ of the Passion and the beatific vision, one might oppose two difficulties drawn from Holy Scripture. The first concerns the prayer of agony in the Garden of Olives (Mt. 26:39): "My Father, if it be possible, let this chalice pass from me. Nevertheless, not as I will but as thou wilt." And the second concerns the dereliction that Christ seems to suffer on the cross (Mt. 27:46): "My God, my God, why hast thou forsaken me?"

---

[147] *Compendium Theologiae*, chap. 232.

It is very interesting to see how St. Thomas replies. To the first difficulty, concerning the prayer of our Lord that the chalice pass from him, yet nonetheless that the will of God be done, he replies:

> Prayer is the expression of desire; therefore it is from the diversity of passions that the motive of the prayer Jesus made before His Passion must come: "My Father, if it be possible, let this chalice pass from me." By saying, "Let this chalice pass from me," Christ expresses the movement of the inferior appetite and the natural desire by which everyone naturally flees death and craves life.[148]

It was the natural desire that our Lord had in Him, as we all have, to not die, to not suffer, to not have our life taken away. This was the experience of the inferior appetite. If He allowed it full expression, it was deliberately, in order to show that He was perfectly a man, and in order to show us and give us an example of the dominion which the superior appetite (the rational will) must have over the natural and sensible appetite:

> By saying, "Nevertheless, not as I will, but as thou wilt," he expresses the movement of the superior reason which considers everything from the angle and under the ordering of divine Wisdom."

The superior appetite consents to the Passion because it is moved by divine Wisdom.

As for the words of the Savior on the cross, "My God, my God, why hast thou forsaken me?" in his commentary on the Gospel according to St. Matthew, St. Thomas explains that they were taken deliberately from Psalm 21, which applies in its entirety to the Passion of Christ. Now, the twenty-first psalm is not a psalm of despair, but rather expresses firm sentiments of hope (v. 25); undoubtedly the

---

[148] *Ibid.*, ch. 233.

Lord appropriated to himself the sentiments of the psalmist. St. Thomas adds:

> If Christ cries out, "My God, why hast thou forsaken me?" it is by way of analogy: Everything we have we have by God. When anyone is exposed to an evil, he describes himself as abandoned; that is why, when God lets a man fall into the evil of sin or of suffering, one speaks of abandonment. That is why Christ speaks of Himself as abandoned, regarding what concerns, not the hypostatic union nor grace, but the Passion.[149]

This dereliction of Christ on the cross is very well explained by Fr. Garrigou-Lagrange, in the line of St. Thomas:

> During the Passion, it was only the summit of the human intellect and will of Jesus that was beatified by the vision of the divine essence, while the less elevated part of His superior faculties and all His sensitive faculties were plunged in suffering at the sight of the sins of men and by the torments of the Passion. (...)[150] The humanity of the Savior was thus like a mountain the summit of which is illuminated by the sun, and looks upon a very calm blue sky, whereas in the less elevated parts the tempest rages and devastates everything.[151]

Let us learn in the school of the Savior to stand fast when undergoing trials whether physical or spiritual, by keeping the summit of our soul unshakably attached to God by faith, hope, and charity.

---

[149] See Rev. Synave, O.P., "*Renseignements techniques sur la Summa Theologica, III, Q. 46-49*," (Ed. *Revue des jeunes*), p. 227.

[150] *Summa Theologica*, III, Q. 46, A. 7, 8.

[151] *L'amour de Dieu et la Croix de Jésus*, (Cerf, 1929), pp. 244-245.

CHAPTER 29

SYNTHESIS OF ALL WISDOM AND KNOWLEDGE

Liberalism and Modernism have penetrated into the most influential and elevated circles of the Church; therefore, measure for measure, let us remain attached to our surest possession, the catechism and theology. We live in an era where, by word or by deed, the highest officials of the Church would limit the omnipotence and the sovereignty of the Lord Jesus Christ. This follows from the fact that you cannot at one and the same time admit that it is possible to be saved without Jesus Christ and affirm His omnipotence. If Jesus Christ is not the only means of salvation, if there are indeed other ways of salvation besides the Lord, then, ultimately, Jesus Christ is not God.

For this reason it is always necessary and good to come back to the Lord and to profess His divinity, and to draw from that fact all its ramifications, bar none.

In the study of the Lord's psychology or interior life, we enter a world where we can never exhaust our admiration for all that is in Him; eternity itself will be spent in the contemplation and joy of knowing Jesus Christ and His divinity. Previously, we described the seeming antinomy existing within our Lord between the beatific vision—the incommensurable and infinite happiness that was His—and His capacity to suffer in both body and soul.

St. Thomas asked the question whether Jesus could suffer, and answered in the affirmative:

> Was Christ's soul passible? As Christ's body was able to suffer and die, as we have said, it necessarily follows that His soul

was for this reason also passible (*Summa Theologica*, III, Q.15, A.4).

In his explanations, St. Thomas always departs from the fact that the human nature that our Lord assumed was perfect, and hence His human soul was perfect and complete. It was not in any way impinged upon by the fact that it was united to the divinity. This is also why St. Thomas tells us that our Lord possessed four different types of knowledge; a fact that is worth knowing and bearing in mind. It is very important.

Firstly, our Lord had divine knowledge, as Word of God contemplating Himself, and contemplating the Father in the Holy Ghost. This knowledge, of course, is absolutely perfect. It is equal to the divine being, and our Lord possessed it because His Person is divine. He also had, in His human soul, the knowledge of the blessed, hence the beatific vision,[152] and this to the utmost degree, since His soul received the *gratia capitis*, the grace suitable for the head of the human race. Jesus Christ is the head of all the elect, the one by whom all knowledge is given to us. He is "He who enlightens every man coming into the world," a passage from the Gospel of St. John read after Mass. Jesus Christ is at the source of the beatific vision possessed by the angels and the blessed in heaven.[153]

It is conceivable that it is He who possesses most perfectly the beatific vision, vision that would have made Him essentially blessed on earth, vision that obliges us to recall the mystery that our Lord, even on the cross, even when He suffered most during the Passion, enjoyed in His soul, in His mind, perfect happiness. It is by the beatific vision

---

[152] *Cf. Summa Theologica*, III, Q.9, A.2.

[153] Namely, the vision face-to-face with God-Trinity, which the souls of the elect in heaven receive as soon as they enter paradise, and which makes them happy.

that our Lord in His human soul is conscious of His divinity, conscious of subsisting in the Person of the Word.

Thirdly, He possesses infused knowledge, which is the natural science of the angels. The angels do not know in the same way we do, by reasoning. Rather, they have ideas, infused concepts, which are given directly to them by God. St. Thomas reaches this conclusion by reasoning thus: Given the perfection of His soul, the Lord was capable of receiving these ideas, these infused concepts, and there was no reason for Him to be deprived of them.[154]

Lastly, our Lord possessed acquired or experimental knowledge. This fact is approached by St. Thomas in the form of a question, for it can really seem inconceivable that Jesus Christ could have had this type of knowledge, as He was already inundated, so to speak, by the three higher forms of knowledge, divine, beatific, and angelic. How then could He have had experimental knowledge.

St. Thomas answers: The Lord had a complete soul, hence He had an "agent intellect," the faculty which abstracts ideas from sensible things. It operates upon the things that we see, and gives us our ideas and all the concepts that we have. This acquired knowledge was possessed by Jesus Christ, too: His understanding would not have been perfect if He had not had this agent intellect capable of acquiring knowledge by means of the things we perceive with our senses,[155] and of knowing the essences of things. Evidently, He already knew these things in another way, so that the acquired knowledge did not add anything new, but it did give Him a new way, another mode of knowing the same things, and to know them concretely as He experienced them.

---

[154] *Op. cit.*, Q.9, A.3.
[155] *Cf. op. cit.*, Q.9, A.4.

This experimental knowledge provides the key to understanding some passages in Scripture. For instance, it is in light of His experimental knowledge that we can understand the words of the Gospel when Joseph and the Virgin Mary went to look for our Lord in the temple and brought Him back to Nazareth: "And Jesus advanced in wisdom and age and grace with God and men" (Lk. 2:52). How, indeed, could He advance in wisdom, since He was perfection itself, if not by the exercise of His agent intellect, by which, in a certain manner, He could grow in experimental knowledge.

It is in this sense, too, that St. Paul says of our Lord and the Passion: "And whereas indeed he was the Son of God, he learned obedience by the things which he suffered" (Heb. 5:8): "*didicit ex iis, quae passus est, obedientiam.*" Here is what St. Thomas has to say:

> He learned obedience, that is to say, how difficult it is to obey, because He had to obey in very grave and difficult things, that is, even unto death....Those who have not experienced obedience, and who have not learned it in carrying out difficult things, believe that obedience is very easy; but for you to learn what it is to obey, you must learn to obey in difficult things (Commentary on Heb. 5).

St. Paul, in the same place, then sets out the meritoriousness of Christ's dolorous experience:

> And being consummated, he became, to all that obey him, the cause of eternal salvation: called by God a high priest, according to the order of Melchisedech (Heb. 5:9,10.).

The idea of St. Paul is that the experimental knowledge of suffering and heroic obedience confer on the Lord a consummation, a particular accomplishment necessary to the exercise of His priesthood. Fr. Lebreton comments:

> The divine knowledge undoubtedly can know our miseries with a sureness and preciseness which no human knowledge can equal, but it knows them in the eternal serenity of a

> contemplation that no suffering has ever caused to tremble. To the Priest and Savior of men another kind of the knowledge of our miseries was necessary, a humbler knowledge, but at the same, more deeply touched; more imperfect, but completely penetrated by human compassion.[156]

These are admirable things. Our Lord is truly the synthesis of all wisdom and all knowledge. He is perfect Wisdom, and we should meditate often on the wisdom of the Lord, and try in the measure possible to pattern our knowledge on His. This we must do by seeking truth by acquired knowledge, by reasoning, by learning new things, and also by the experience of the trials and tribulations of life. Yet we also do this by faith, by the adhesion of our minds to revealed truths; and still more by the gift of wisdom which enables us to judge things as our Lord does: then we would be approaching the infused knowledge which angels have, because it consists of lights, ideas given by God himself. Faith is nothing other than a preparation for the beatific vision. It already includes all the truths which shall make us eternally happy. Hence our need to ask the good God that we may know our faith and live it faithfully and fully, so that we may begin to participate even now, to a certain degree, in the beatific vision.

These are considerations that afford much consolation, and we should think of them often. It is by so doing that we shall acquire an ever greater union to the truth that is our Lord Jesus Christ Himself: "I am the way, the truth and the life" (Jn. 14:6).

If we, too, desire to abide in the truth, we must, again, I say, take our Lord as our model, and ask Him to keep us steadfast in the truth.

---

[156] J. Lebreton, *Histoire du dogme de la Trinité*, 7th ed., Vol. 1, 1927, p.456, cited by Rev. Médébielle, S.C.N., *Commentaire de l'épître aux Hébreux* in *La Sainte Bible*, published under the direction of Louis Pirot, Vol. XII, p.312.